CRY.

Christians Reason Yourself.

AZEEZ UR RAHMAN

*Dedicated to mankind and all universal intelligent beings,
and published with a fervent prayer; for, it is
a nail shod in this heart of mine.
Amen.*

CONTENTS

Reference for religious quotes used in this book:

The Holy Bible
King James Version copyright 1982 by Thomas Nelson, Inc. 'The Bible: Book for All Time' from a Reader's Guide to the Holy Bible revised edition copyright 1972–1983 by Thomas Nelson Inc.

The Holy Quran
Text translation and commentary by Abdullah Yusuf Ali, Volume 1 & ll combined. Kutub Khana Ishayat-ul-Islam (Regd). 3755 Churiwalan, Delhi–110006, INDIA. 4th Edition 1989.
Hadia: Ref. No. 10, Volume 1 & 2.

FOREWORD

Bismillah hir Rahmaanir Raheem
In the name of ALLAH (God)
the Beneficent, the Merciful

The author does not take credit for the knowledge and teachings in this book. He has merely collated the material here, primarily from English translations of the Holy Quran. He owes much to the thinkers whose writings have led him to this book, and of course, to the author of authors, God, who has revealed the Holy Quran.

It was inspired by a keen need to understand our world through reasoning and rationalism.

There are some statements and quotes from the Holy Bible and the Holy Quran that have been repeated in this book on purpose to lay stress on them. This has been done so that the reader may be reminded again and again, in the hope that such repeated reflection will help arrive at the right understanding with one's God-given reasoning faculty.

Dear reader, before you start on your journey of discovery, here is a prayer for you. May reason dictate your path to God's plan for you and may you find your place in God's Universal Computer Program!

May Allah (God)[1] make
Wisdom, your capital
Reason, the force of your religion
Love, your foundation
Longing, your vehicle
Remembrance of Allah, your constant pleasure
Trust, your treasure
Mourning, your companion
Knowledge, your arm
Patience, your robe
Conviction, your strength
Holy war, your ethics
Contentment, your booty
Poverty, your pride
Asceticism, your profession
Truthfulness, your intercessor
Obedience, your argument
Prayers, your supreme pleasure.
Amen.

---

[1] A proper name has to be the same in any language. Therefore, the author uses 'Allah', the Arabic name of the Supreme Being as well as 'God', which is better understood in English. He is the one and only, unique God. Jesus spoke Aramic and called God 'Elah' which is pronounced the same as 'Allah'. Aramic is an ancient, biblical language. It is one of the Semitic languages that also includes Hebrew, Arabic, Ethiopic and the ancient Assyrian and Babylon language of Akkadian. The Aramic 'Elah' and the Arabic 'Allah' are the same. The Aramic 'Elah' is derived from the Arabic 'Allah', and it means 'God', the Supreme God Almighty. You can easily see the similarity in their pronunciation. So it would be reasonable to use the proper name 'Allah' instead of God in this book. However the word 'God' in English can be written/printed with a small 'g', it can be conjugated into god, gods, or goddess, and goddesses. All this is improper. Your name printed in any language still remains the same. Hence 'Allah' is the proper name of the Supreme Being. However 'God' is used in this book for reasons as explained earlier.

This book is dedicated firstly to the followers of The Book i.e. Christians, as we have been instructed to teach, first to those nearest to Islam, and also to the Jews and all others.

Refer HQ 5:85 "Strongest among men in enmity to the Believers will you find the Jews and Pagans, and the nearest among them in love to the Believers will you find those who say, 'we are Christians.'"

Hence, this book on Islam is first meant for Christians, then next, to men of all other faiths including Muslims. Allah has not created anything better than Reason; or anything more perfect or more beautiful than Reason, the benefits of which God has given are on its account, and understanding is by it. God's wrath is caused by disregard of it. Therefore, dear reader, proceed only with your reason. The Quran gives great importance to the faculty of reason. Several verses in the Quran emphasize the importance of rational thinking. Here is a translation of a related verse: HQ8:22 "The worst creatures in Allah's eyes are those who are deaf and dumb, and who do not use their reason."

What is reason? Reason is the power of the mind to think, analyze and form judgements in a logical manner. It is the most powerful faculty and distinctive quality of a human being.

Reason is not an isolated faculty. According to the Quran, the whole of creation is based on reason. The religion revealed by God is also a rational religion. Every one is required to plan one's life using reason. Those failing to do so are considered deaf, dumb and blind. Only that belief is valid which is based on reason and understanding.

Reason is what makes man a rational animal. Man has a mind with boundless capacity, and is like a hidden treasure. It is his first duty to unfold this potential. Dying without unfolding one's intellectual potential, is to die like an animal. Such a person fails to fulfill the creation plan of Allah.

HQ18:54 "We have explained in detail in this Quran, for the benefit of mankind, every kind of similitude: but man is, in most things contentious."

If men had not cultivated the habit of contention and obstinacy, they would have found that the parables and similitude of Scripture had fully met their difficulties, and they would have gladly obeyed the call of God.

HQ39:27 "We have put forth for men, in this Quran every kind of parable in order that they may receive admonition."

Men can only understand high spiritual truths, by parables and similitude and these are given abundantly in the Quran. The object is not merely to tell stories, but to teach lessons of spiritual wisdom.

Having read so far let us get down to basics. Let us understand the basic meanings of the words, 'Logic' and 'Reason', and their derivatives being used in this book, as everything depends on them. If you do not understand or disagree with something in this book, then get back to Chapter 1, and let your reason decide for you.

Chapter 1

FAITH, LOGIC AND REASON

All your life, from childhood to the present day, you have been using God's gift—the wonderful, awesome human brain. For your whole life you have used the reasoning power of your brain. However, for belief in religion you use only faith. Why? The same analogy must be used for life as well.

How come you do not use this same 'reasoning power' faculty of the brain to identify the One and Only True Religion—the same taught by all prophets—Abraham, Moses, Jesus, Isaac, and Mohammed. There are many more prophets not mentioned in the Holy Quran, and many more of whom we do not know. May Peace and the Blessing of God be on them all.

Let us get down to the basics of Logic and Reason. This whole book is based on these two words and their derivatives along with the associated words.

Firstly, let us understand the meaning of these words as given in the dictionary:

Funk & Wagnalls dictionary defines:

Faith (noun)

A firm conviction of the truth of what is declared by another by way either of testimony, or authority, without other evidence.

Specifically in theology. The assent of the mind or understanding to the truth of what God has revealed; belief in the testimony of God as contained in the scriptures.

Reason (both verb and noun)

(a). That which is supposed or affirmed to support or justify any conclusion, belief, or plan of action; a fact, truth, or end to be attained; which serves the mind as a rational ground or motive, proof for an opinion, judgement, or resolution; principle of thought or action.

(b) That which explains or accounts for any thing or event.

(c) The group of faculties, attributes, or activities which distinguishes man as a so-called rational animal from the brutes.

Two heads:

Logical understanding — or discursive reason, which makes man capable of learning and of scientific achievements, as the lower animals are not.

A collective term for the so-called a-priori constitution of thought and the capacity of framing and following ethical, aesthetic and religious ideals, of which the lower animals show few, or no traces.

Rational (adjective)

Endowed with reason, reasoning, sensible, sane, based on derived form, reason or reasoning, not foolish, absurd or extravagant.

Rationalism (noun)

Treating reason as the ultimate authority in religion as elsewhere. Theory that reason is foundation of certainty in knowledge.

Ratiocinate (intransitive verb)

Reason, carry on process of reasoning.

Logic (noun)

The science or doctrine of correct thinking; the principles governing the reasoning faculties in the pursuit and exposition of truth.

Proof (noun)

The art or process of proving in any sense specific.

1. The establishment of a fact by evidence or a truth by other truths.

2. A trial of strength or excellence, a test; as, the proof of a musket.

Now after having understood the meanings of the words, Reason and its derivatives, Faith and Logic, dear reader delve into this poor surmise of the Quran. Better still delve into the Quran, to understand yourself and the reason for your being in this world for a short time. Human beings use logic to understand everything in life but are unable to use the same logic for the existence of God, the life hereafter, the truth and religion. Why is this so?

The British philosopher Bertrand Russell has rightly pointed out that knowledge is of two kinds: Knowledge of Things and Knowledge of Truth. Both these arguments are valid. People do not know the difference between these two subjects; they try to apply logic that pertains to the first category (i.e. Things) to the second category (i.e. Truth). This wrong application leads to confusion. Now that we have understood the meaning of the basic words, then, by reason, 'Christian' means the true followers of Prophet Jesus Christ.

This includes:

(a) True Christians – i.e. those who believe and follow the 'Red Letter Bible', that is all Loggia i.e. sayings of Jesus Christ recorded in the gospels and also not recorded but preserved elsewhere, and not what was written by Saints Matthew, Mark, Luke and John, and others about Jesus, long after his death.

Nor can the followers of the Nicene creed propounded by the NICEA Council in AD 325, which annunciated

Trinity be called 'Christians'. Logically they should be called 'Trinitarians' (i.e. those believing in the Trinity) or 'Nicene Councilists'.

(b) All true Muslims who must believe in Jesus and all that was preached and said by him are true Christians. Refer HQ2:4 and 42:13.

This is what God says in the Quran as to who is a Christian.

HQ3:55 says: "Behold! God said 'O Jesus! I will take thee and raise thee to Myself and clear thee of the falsehood of those who (a) blaspheme; I will make those who follow thee superior to those who (b) reject faith'..."

Jesus was charged by the Jews with blasphemy in claiming to be God or the Son of God. The Christians except a few early sects which were annihilated by persecution and the modern sect of Unitarians, who are almost Muslims, adopted the substance of the claim and made it the cornerstone of their faith. God clears Jesus of such a charge or claim.

'Those who follow thee': Muslims are true Christians for they follow the true teaching of Jesus Christ which did not include the blasphemy that he was God. Or the Son of God in the literal sense. But there is a large body of men who by birth inherit such teaching nominally. However their hearts do not consent to it, obviously by reason. Their real Muslim virtues (which from their point of view they call Christian virtues) entitle them to be called Christians, and to receive the leading position which they at present occupy in the world of men.

The Quran gives great importance to the faculty of reason. Several verses in the Quran emphasize the importance of rational thinking. Here is a translation of a related verse HQ8:22, "The worst creatures in God's eyes are those who are deaf and dumb, and who do not use their reason."

Again, what is reason? Reason is the power of the mind to think, analyze and form judgements in a logical manner. It is the most powerful faculty and a distinctive quality of a human being. Reason is not an isolated faculty. According to the Quran, the whole of creation is based on reason. The religion revealed by God is also a rational religion. Everyone is required to plan one's life using reason. Those failing to do so are considered deaf, dumb and blind. Only that belief is valid which is based on reason and understanding.

Reason is what makes man a rational animal. Man has a mind with boundless capacity, and is like a hidden treasure. It is his first duty to unfold this potential. Dying without unfolding one's intellectual potential, is to be like an animal. Such a person fails to fulfil the creation plan of God. Reason needs to be developed.

The Quran mentions several methods for this intellectual development—study, contemplation, observation, taking lessons from experiences, etc. Every individual must inculcate the spirit of learning. This will consistently improve one's personality.

Reason cannot be created but it can certainly be developed. Everyone has a twofold duty of developing his reason or mind, and then using it in life. Reason is a powerful ability of the human mind, and we are duty-bound to turn this potential into actuality.

The Quran says that reason has both positive and negative outcomes. When used with sincerity and modesty, it serves as a constructive and healthy part of one's personality. But if one is a victim of egoism, then reason makes him an arrogant person and that is a negative outcome.

Understanding the Quran or any other religious book, requires deep contemplation. Without applying reason, no one can contemplate. On reading the Quran one will find that it always addresses reason. Reason is the master key to a better understanding of all human issues.

Chapter 2

ONE GOD, ONE TRUTH, ONE RELIGION

The Message revealed through all prophets is a universal Message. It cannot be different at different ages/time, to human beings on earth, just as the miracle of water is the same all around the world; it is the same H_2O. Can our Lord's Message be different, to different people, at different times? His Message excludes no one—rich or poor, old or young, great or lowly, learned or ignorant. If anyone has a spiritual craving that needed to be satisfied, he is to be given precedence if there is to be any question of precedence at all.

HQ29:49: "In this Book are signs self-evident in the hearts of those endowed with knowledge….".

Knowledge means both power of judgement in discerning the value of truth and acquaintance with previous revelations. It implies both literary and spiritual insight. To men so endowed, God's revelation and signs are self-evident. They commend themselves to these men's hearts, minds, and understanding.

Divine knowledge is a fathomless ocean. But glimpses of it can be obtained by any individual sincerely searching for the truth. This progress will be in grades. If they ask questions, and answers are then furnished to them, they are more likely to apprehend the Truth, as they have already explored the part of the territory in which they are interested. In the same way, when concrete questions arise by the turn of events, and they are answered not only for the occasion, but from a general standpoint, teaching has a far greater chance of penetrating the human intelligence and taking shape in practical conduct. And this is the usual way of instruction in the Quran.

It is not for the author to force any one to accept the Truth which he is told and inspired to preach or proclaim. A man's actual personal religion depends upon many things—his psychological make-up, the background of his life, his hidden or repressed feelings, tendencies, or history (which psychoanalysis tries to unravel), his hereditary disposition, antipathies and all the subtle influences of his education and environment. The task before the man of Allah (God) is:

(a) to use any of these which can serve the higher ends

(b) to purify such as have been misused

(c) to introduce new ideas and modes of looking at things

(d) to combat what is wrong and try to mend the same

All for the purpose of leading to the Truth and gradually letting in spiritual light where there was darkness before. If that is not done with discretion and the skill of a spiritual teacher, there may be not only an obstinate reaction, but an unseemly show of dishonour to God and His Truth, and doubts would spread among the weaker brethren whose path is shallow and infirm. What happens to individuals is true collectively, of nations or groups of people. They think in their self- obsession that their own ideas are right.

God in His infinite compassion bears with them, and asks those who have purer ideas of faith not to vilify the weaknesses of their neighbours, lest the neighbours in their turn vilify the real Truth and make matters worse than before. In so far as there is active evil, God will deal with it in His own way. Of course the righteous man must not hide his light under a bushel or compromise with evil, or refuse to establish right living where he has the power to do so.

The transparent crystal Truth you may yet mistake for the unstable water of worldly vanity, which soils the vestments of those who paddle in it. This leads one to many undignified positions and mistakes, but a reader who considers, is mindful and understands by reasoning points out the truth instead of resenting it.

God has promised through the law of all His revelations which includes the Gospels, the Taurat,[2] the Quran and other Books/Revelations which we do not know as a promise binding on Him. "…And who is more faithful to His covenant than God?…" HQ9:111. We should offer our whole selves and our possessions to God, and He will give us salvation, i.e. eternal freedom from bondage of this world. This is the true doctrine of redemption, and we are taught that this is the doctrine not only of the Quran but of all the earlier revelations: the original Law of Moses, and the original Gospel of Jesus.

Any other view of redemption should be rejected by all reasoning and right-thinking individuals. The Christian concept of redemption as believed in Christianity where some other person suffered for our sins and we are redeemed by his blood, must be rejected. It is our self-surrender that counts, not other peoples' merits. Our complete self-surrender may include fighting for the cause, both spiritual and physical. Is God so unmindful that all those human beings who died/ passed away before Jesus Christ and the doctrine of salvation only through baptism established thereafter, are all going to Hell?

"…All men are in debt for their deeds on this earth." HQ52:21

HQ3:81. The Quran says "Behold God took the covenant of the prophets (Prophet Moses) saying, 'I give you a book

---

[2] 1. (see Appendix I and II)

and Wisdom, then comes to you an apostle, confirming what is with you. Do ye believe in him and render him help'. God said, 'Do ye agree and take My covenant as binding on you?' They said, 'We agree' He said, 'Then bear witness, I am with you among the witnesses'." The argument is—you People of the Book (Jews and Christians) are bound by your own oaths sworn solemnly in the presence of your own prophets.

In the OT (Old Testament) as it now exists, Prophet Muhammad is foretold in Duet. 18:18. In the New Testament, as it now exists, Prophet Muhammad is foretold in the Gospel of St. John 14:16, 15:26 and 16:7. The future comforter cannot be the Holy Spirit as understood by Christians, because the Holy Spirit already was present, helping and guiding Christ. The Greek word translated for 'Comforter' is Paracletos – meaning Advocate i.e. one called to the help of another. This word 'Paracletos' is an easy corruption from 'Periclytos' meaning 'The praised one' which is almost the literal translation of Muhammad or Ahmed, meaning 'The praised one'.

Further, there were/are other Gospels that have perished, but of which traces still remain, which were even more specific in their reference to prophet Muhammad. See the Gospel of Barnabas, of which an Italian translation is extant in the State Library of Vienna. It was edited in 1907 with an English translation by Mr. Lonsdale and Laura Ragg. God's Love is inescapable as nature's environment, which if a man ignores or think to thrust it off, he is the ill-natured fool that runneth blindly on to death. All nature adores God, and Islam asks for nothing peculiar or sectarian, it but asks that we follow our nature and make our will conformable to God's Will as seen in nature and Revelations. Its message is universal.

You, people of the Book i.e. Christians and Jews, do not hate or disassociate yourselves from us Muslims just because we believe in God, and not only our scripture (The Holy Quran) but yours also. It may be because we obey the one and only true religion revealed since beginning of time, from the One and Only God, to all mankind, and you are in rebellion against God. People of your faith rebelled against God and the treatment meted out by God and incurred the curse of God. Please read Duet. 11:28 and 28:15-68; also Hosea 8:14 and 9:1.

Who provoked Allah's wrath? Please read Duet. 1:34, Matt.3:7. Who forsook Allah (God) and worshipped evil? Please read Jeremiah 16:11-13.

HQ84: 20-25 "What then is the matter with them (People of the Book) that they believe not? And when the Quran is read to them, they fall not prostrate, but on the contrary the unbelievers reject it. But God has full knowledge of what they secrete in their breasts.

So announce to them a Penalty Grievous, except to those who believe and work righteous deeds; for them is a reward that will never fail."

Considering man's high destiny, and the fact that this life is but a stage or a sojourn for him, it might be expected that he would eagerly embrace every opportunity of welcoming God's Revelation and ascending by faith to heights of spiritual wisdom. There is something wrong with his will if he does not do so. What does your reason say?

Islam (surrender of oneself to the will and purpose of God) existed before the preaching of Muhammad on this earth. The Quran expressly calls Prophet Abraham a Muslim. HQ3:67.

Its teaching 'Submission to Allah's Will' has been and will be the teaching of religion for all time and all peoples—that is to the whole world/universe.

The path of Islam is simple and easy. It depends on no abstruse mysteries or self-mortifications, but on straight and manly conduct in accordance with the laws of man's nature as implanted in him by God.

HQ30:30. "So set thou thy face solidly & truly to the Faith: (Establish) God's handiwork according to the pattern on which He has made mankind. No change (let there be) in the work (wrought). By God, that is the Standard Religion. But most among mankind understand not."

On the other hand, spiritual perfection may be most difficult, for it involves complete surrender on our part to God in all our affairs, thoughts and desires; but after that surrender, God's Grace will make our path easy.

HQ87:8-11 says "And We will make it easy for thee to follow the simple Path."

"Therefore, give admonition where the admonition profits the hearer. The admonition will be received by those who fear God. But it will be avoided by those most unfortunate ones."

The doctrine of personal responsibility is the cardinal feature of Islam. If one believes in a soul at all, the very foundation of religion, then one must believe in a future after death, without which the soul has no meaning.

God's Truth is manifest, and all that is good and true and sane and normal. Men of understanding should accept it with joy. But even where there is a disease in the heart or judgement is obscured by perversity, every creature must eventually see and acknowledge God and His Power.

"For God's love is as inescapable as nature's environment, which if a man ignores or thinks to thrust it off, he is the ill-natured fool that runneth blindly on to death." (R. Bridges— Testament of Beauty.)

All Nature adores God and Islam asks for nothing peculiar or sectarian; it but asks that we follow our nature and make our will conformable to God's will as seen in nature, History, Revelation and in one's Reasoning. Its message is universal.

Thus Islam's position is clear. Islam does not claim to have a religion peculiar to itself. Islam is not a sect or an ethnic religion. In its view all religion is one, for the Truth is one. It was and is the religion preached by all the earlier Prophets. It was the Truth taught by all the Inspired Books.

In essence it amounts to a consciousness of the Will and Plan of God and a joyful submission to that Will and Plan. If any one wants a religion other than that, he is false to his own nature, as he is false to God's Will and Plan. Such a person cannot expect guidance, for he has deliberately renounced guidance.

Islamic Creed — (a) HQ2:136, (b)3:84.

(a) HQ2:136 . "Say ye, We believe in Allah,(God) and the revelation given to Abraham, Ismail, Isaac, Jacob, and the Tribes, and that given to Moses and Jesus, and that given to all prophets, from their Lord. We make no difference between one and another of them, and we bow to Allah (God) in Islam."

In the two verses mentioned, the common sentence is 'We make no difference between all the Prophets'. All were Messengers of Allah and all taught the same lesson to one class, the world.

(b). HQ3:84 This is 99% same as above.

HQ41:43 "Nothing is said to thee (Prophet Muhammad) that was not said to the apostles before thee…"

Earlier Revelations came to all the Prophets in the world to each tribe, continent, people community and race. All Revelations came from one God. All revelations had to be in essence the same. One Teacher—God, one class for mankind – the world. The last revelation—the Holy Quran—came at a time when mankind had much knowledge to accurately note down the same and retain it in books and in memory.

It is the last revelation by human reasoning as the world, that is the continents, countries, islands, and cities were at that time in communication with each other with various modes of transport – ships, caravans, animal drawn carts; and in time, various other means like radio waves, telephones, telegrams and computers. Hence by reason further revelations by God were not needed as the same age-old lesson—Revelation of God could be communicated to the whole world.

The Quran is the only Revelation with 114 chapters and 6238 verses which is known by heart by millions of Muslims. The Quran presents itself as 'easy to understand and remember'.

All the 114 chapters are in both poetic and prose form—mind you, in Arabic—not in English, or any other language/translation.

The Quran inspires and teaches us what is to be taught, why and how.

HQ39:41 "…Verily We have revealed the book to thee for instructing mankind. He then that receives guidance benefits his own soul, but he that strays injures his own soul."

HQ7:2 "A book revealed unto thee (Prophet Muhammad), so let thy heart be oppressed no more by any difficulty on that account that with it thou mightiest warn the erring and teach the believers."

If we seek God's help we must first help God's cause, that is dedicate ourselves to Him entirely and without reserve. This was also the teaching of Jesus, as mentioned in the verse above.

As found in the New Testament, the metaphor used is that of the cross. "Then said Jesus to his disciples: if any man will come to me, let him deny himself and take up the cross, and follow me" (Matt. 16:24) Similarly HQ61:14—as said Jesus, son of Mary to the disciples "Who will be my helpers to the work of God?"

Refer HQ3:85. The Muslim position is clear. The Muslim does not claim to have a religion, peculiar to himself. Islam is not a sect or an ethnic religion. In its view all Religion is one, for the Truth is one. It was the religion preached by all the earlier Prophets. It was the Truth taught by all the Inspired Books. In essence it amounts to a consciousness of the Will and Plan of God and a joyful submission to that Will and Plan. If anyone wants a religion other than that, he is false to his own nature, as he is false to God's Will and Plan. Such a person cannot expect guidance for he has deliberately renounced guidance.

The highest issues for man hang on his behaviour in his short life on earth. Life is real, life is earnest. The grave is not its goal. We must therefore earnestly search out God's Truth, encouraged by the fact that God's Truth is also out of His unbounded Mercy, searching us out and trying to reach us.

There is an implied covenant among all created things/ beings to follow God's law, which is the law of their being, in that we should carry out our obligation/ mission proclaiming God's Truth, without fear or favour and be ever ready in His service in all circumstances.

First, there are the divine obligations that arise from our nature and our relation to God. He created us and implanted in us the faculty of knowledge and foresight; besides the intuition and reason which He gave us. He made nature responsive to our needs, and His signs in nature are so many lessons to us in our own inner life; He further sent Messengers and Teachers, for the guidance of our conduct in individual, social, and public life. All these gifts create corresponding obligations which we must fulfill. But in our own human and material life we undertake mutual obligations, express and implied. We make a promise; we enter into a commercial or social contract; we enter into a contract of marriage; we must faithfully fulfil all obligations in all these relationships.

Our group or our state enters into a treaty; every individual in that group or state is bound to see that, as far as lies in his power, such obligations are faithfully discharged.

There are tacit obligations: living in civil society, we must respect its tacit convention unless they are morally wrong and in that case we must get out of such society. There are tacit obligations in the characters of host and guest, wayfarer or companion, employer or employed etc., which every man of Faith must discharge conscientiously.

The man who deserts those who need him and goes to pray in a desert is a coward who disregards his obligations. All these obligations are interconnected. Truth and fidelity are parts of religion in all relationships of life.

There is nothing more certain in the world, physical moral, and spiritual, than that every cause, great or small, must have its corresponding consequences.

Chapter 3

DEFINITION OF ISLAM

HQ 2:136. "We believe in God and the revelation given to us, and to Abraham, Ismail, Isaac, Jacob and the tribes and that given to Moses and Jesus and that given to (all) Prophets from their Lord. We make no difference between one and another of them: and we bow to God in Islam."

HQ 29:46. "We believe in the Revelation which has come down to us in that which came down to you, (Jews and Christians); our God and your God is One, and it is to Him we bow down in Islam." That is surrender ourselves to His Will and Purpose.

All Muslims are Christians, as they believe without doubt in Jesus Christ and in all that he said/preached, that is the ' Red Letter Bible'. However, they do not believe in what was said/written about Jesus Christ by Saints Matthew, Mark, Luke and John; that too, long after Jesus was dead/ passed away/ crucified.

Islam from the root word 'Salaam' in Arabic means Peace.

Islam, the religion of Muslims, means 'surrender of oneself to the Will and Purpose of God'. The God whom it preaches about is not an exclusive God. He is the Lord of the Worlds (i.e. the universe) to any given person, of whatever faith, He is your God as well as mine.

What cause of contention whatever can one have when we preach Unity, Truth, and the Hereafter?

HQ30:58. "Every kind of parable, example or lesson is ...propounded for men in the Quran, but if any Sign is given the unbelievers are sure to say: 'Ye do nothing but talk vanities.'"

Things of the highest moment have been explained in the Quran from various points of view; by means of parables; and similitude drawn from nature and from ordinary daily life, but whatever the explanation, however convincing it may be to men who earnestly seek the Truth, those who deliberately turn their backs to Truth can find nothing convincing. In their eyes, the explanations are 'vain talk' or false arguments.

Only men make mistakes. Allah (God) does not and cannot make a mistake. Therefore, from the beginning of creation Allah has sent down the same Advice, Warning, Truth, The Straight Way, Revelation through many apostles, messengers and prophets, generally known the world over as Religion, so it has to be the same. Mankind has altered/corrupted the True Message for his advantage, due to greed, pride, conceit, or lost/burnt due to negligence, except the Quran, which claims to be pure. God will protect it from corruption. The Quran says so itself :"It is easy to understand and remember." The last revealed Book which was a Code of Life was the Book of Moses; for that of Jesus was not such a Code, but merely moral precepts to sweep away the corruptions that had crept in. The Quran has the same attitude to it as the teaching of Jesus had to the Law.

Jesus said (Matt.5:17) "Think not that I am came to destroy the Law or the Prophets; I did not come to destroy, but to fulfil." But the corruptions took new forms in Christian Churches: an entirely new Code became necessary, and this was provided in Islam.

The logical conclusion to the evolution of religious history is a non-sectarian, non-racial, non-doctrinal, universal religion, which Islam claims to be.

For Islam is just submission to the Will of Allah (God). This implies (1) Faith, (2) Doing right; being an example to others to do right, and having the power to see that right prevails, (3) Eschewing wrong, being an example to others to eschew wrong, and having the power to see that wrong and injustice are defeated. Islam therefore lives, not for itself, but for mankind. The People of the Book, if only they had faith, would be Muslim, for they have been prepared for Islam.

Unfortunately, there is Unfaith, but it can never harm those who carry the banner of Faith and Right, which must always be victorious.

Chapter 4

WHY PREACH ISLAM?

Why should we Muslims, followers of Prophet Jesus, Moses, Abraham, and all other prophets preach about Islam 'Peace'?

If we men seek God's help, we must first help God's cause i.e., dedicate ourselves to Him entirely and without reserve.

This was also the teaching of Jesus, son of Mary, as mentioned in the HQ 61:14. "O ye who believe! Be helpers of God." As said Jesus, son of Mary, to the Disciples, "Who will be my helpers to the work of God?"

The same is mentioned in the New Testament—Matt 16:24 "Then said Jesus to his disciples, if any man desires to come after me let him deny himself, and take up his cross, and follow me." The metaphor is that of the cross, for teaching/being helpers of God's cause.

It is the duty of every man, woman, or child to read and understand it according to his own capacity. If any one of us attains to some knowledge of understanding of it by study, contemplation and the test of life both outward and inward, it is his duty, according to his capacity, to instruct others and share with them the joy and peace which results from contact with the spiritual world. The Quran indeed every uncorrupted, religious book has to be the same; that is, give the same instructions/lessons by the One and Only Master—God, to one class—The World, and has to be read not only with the tongue and voice and eyes, but with the best light that our intellect can supply, and even more, with the truest and purest light which our heart and conscience and reasoning can give us. It is in this spirit that one should approach the Quran.

HQ39:41. "Verily We have revealed the book to thee in Truth for instructing mankind. He then that receives guidance benefits his own soul; But he that strays, injures his own soul…"

HQ7:2. "A book revealed unto thee – that with it thou mightest warn the erring and teach the Believers." HQ103: 1-3. "By the token of time through the ages verily man is in loss, except as have Faith, and do righteous deeds and join together in the mutual teaching of Truth, and of patience and constancy."

HQ39:33. "And he who brings the Truth and he who confirms and supports it, such are the men who do right."

HQ51:55,56. "But teach, for teaching benefits the believers."

Refer to HQ3:20. We Muslims are asked to say to the People of the Book and to those who are unlearned — 'Do you submit yourselves to the Will and Purpose of God? But if they turn away, our duty is to convey the message'.

Ever this eternal light of Unity, this mystique of God's Will has shone and shines with undiminished splendour. The names of many messengers are inscribed in the records of many nations and many tongues, and many were the forms in which their one and only Message was delivered according to the need of the times and the understanding of the people; And manifold also was the response of their people; but they all bore witness to the One Truth of God's Unity, Might, Grace and Love.

As the records of man are imperfect, and the memory of man unstable, the names of many of the messengers are known in one place and not in another, or among one people and not among others, and some of their names may have perished utterly. But their message stands indivisible, even though it may have been forgotten, or twisted by ignorance, error, superstition or perversity. Or even misunderstanding in the blinding light of time or tortuous circumstances.

Many were the faiths in the composite world of Western Asia, Northern Africa, and Europe and many were the fragments of ancient wisdom, saved, transformed, renewed, or mingled; and many new systems of wisdom were poured through the crucibles of noble minds—prophets, poets, preachers, philosophers, and thinking men of action; Many were the conflicts and many were the subtle influences interchanged with the other worlds further than Eastern Asia, and perchance with the scattered islands of the Pacific and the world between the Atlantic and the Pacific Oceans.

God's decree is known to us by logic, facts and reasoning. No thinking mind, if it only judges the matter fairly, can fail to find the truth of what has been revealed to all prophets and through Nature—the unity of God in his own heart and conscience.

Clear signs have come from Revelations by all prophets, from your own conscience, and from all nature around you.

"…No want of proportion wilt thou see in the Creation of God most Gracious. So turn thy vision again, seest thou any flaw?" HQ 67:3

Just think of your wrist, thumb and fingers, how they have served you throughout your life. Have you picked up just the right thing wanted from your pocket or purse without looking in?

"Again turn thy vision a second time. Thy vision will come back to thee dull and discomfited in a state worn out." HQ67:4. In other words, Nature is perfect.

The fire of God's test, either by adversity or by affluence, will search out the true metal in us and reject the dross which we collect from all sorts of scum and vanity which we call knowledge.

HQ29:18."And if you reject this Message so did generations before you. The duty of the apostle is only to preach publicly and clearly."

HQ29:46."And dispute ye not with the People of the Book, except with means better than mere disputations— and say we believe in the revelation which has come down to us and in that which has come down to you; our God and your God is One; and it is to Him we bow in Islam."

To whom, how and why should the Latest Message be informed? The Quran answers: To whom?

Refer HQ5:85 Nearest to the Believers i.e. Christians because among them are men devoted to learning, who have renounced the world and they are not arrogant.

How?

HQ29:46 "…with means better" and 4:63: "Speak to them in such terms as will address their minds."

Why?

Because Islam is 'the Standard Religion'. HQ30:30.

By Time. HQ103:3. "Verily man is in loss, except such as have faith and do righteous deeds and in the mutual teaching of truth and patience and constancy."

Further, God says HQ75:16-19. "Move not thy tongue concerning the Quran to make haste therewith. It is for Us to collect it and to promulgate it, follow thee its recital (as promulgated). Nay, more it is for Us to explain it…"

Further, HQ2:106 "None of Our revelations do We abrogate or cause to be forgotten, but We substitute something better or similar. Knowest thou not that God hath power over all things?"

Chapter 5

THE HOLY QURAN

Allah (God) has made One Universal Computer Program for the universe. Therefore, there has to be only one religion from the beginning of time, as there is only One God.

HQ 87:18-19 "And this the Holy Quran … is in the Books of earliest revelations, the Books of Abraham and Moses."

No Book of Abraham has come down to us. But the old testaments recognize that Abraham was a prophet. (Ref. Gen 20:7). There is a book in Greek which has been translated by Mr. G. H. Box, called The Testament of Abraham (published by the Society for the Promotion of Christian Knowledge, London 1927).

It seems to be a Greek translation of a Hebrew original. The Greek text was probably written in the second Christian century in Egypt, but in its present form it probably goes back only to the 9th or 10th century. It was popular among the Christians. Perhaps the Jewish Midrash also refers to a Testament of Abraham. It also appears in the original Revelation of Moses, of which the present Pentateuch is a surviving recension.

The present Gospels do not come under the definition of the 'earliest' Books. Nor could they be called 'Books of Jesus'; they were written not by him, but about him, and long after his death.

"… and there never was a people without a Warner, having lived among them in the past." (HQ35:24).

God's Truth is manifest, and all that is good and true, sane and normal which one with reason should accept with joy. But even where there is a disease in the heart (HQ2:10), or judgement obscured by perversity every creature must eventually see and acknowledge God and His power. Compare R. Bridges' Testament of Beauty — "For God's love is as inescapable as nature's environment; which if a man ignore or think to thrust it off, he is the ill-natured fool that runneth blindly on to death." All nature adores God, and Islam asks nothing peculiar or sectarian; it but asks that we follow our nature and make our will conformable to God's will as seen in nature, history, and revelation. Its Message has to be and is universal.

HQ 2:136

We Muslims have been ordered to/told to/asked to say: "We believe in God and the revelations given to us, and to Abraham, Ismail, Isaac, Jacob, and the tribes and that given to Moses and Jesus, and that given to all Prophets from their Lord. We make no difference between one and another of them, and we bow to God in Islam."

Again, a similar verse HQ3:84. In these two verses quoted above we have the creed of Islam to believe in

1. The One Universal God.

2. The Message to us all, through Prophet Muhammad and the signs, that is the Quran as interpreted on the basis of personal responsibility.

3. The Message delivered by other Teachers / Prophets in the past. These are mentioned in three groups:

a) Abraham, Ismail, Jacob, and other Tribes: of these Abraham apparently had a book (as mentioned in the Quran 87:19) and the others followed his tradition.

b) Moses and Jesus, who each left a scripture; these scriptures are still extant though not in their pristine form.

c) There are other scriptures, Prophets or Messengers of God, not specifically mentioned in the Quran and "we make no difference between any of them". Refer HQ 4:152.

One Teacher, God; One class, the World – maybe the whole Universe; One Lesson, Islam — meaning The Surrender of oneself to the Will and Purpose of God.

HQ 50:37 "Verily in the Quran is a message for any that has a heart and understanding, or who gives ear and earnestly witnesses the Truth". As Jesus said (Matt 11:15), "He that hath ears to hear, let him hear." These are matters of high moment. Many spiritual lessons can be learned from these things by anyone who has the heart and understanding to apply God's teaching and can give genuine thought to what he sees as a witness does, to swear to the facts on oath.

HQ 46:2 "The revelation of the Book (Quran) is from God the exalted in Power, full of Wisdom". When God bestow favours on man he turns away. And when evil seizes him, he comes full of prolonged prayer. Therefore, come to God with your reasoning, the favour bestowed on you by Him.

HQ 44:58: "Verily, We have made this (Quran) easy, in thy tongue, in order that they may give heed."

Further, the Quran says in HQ 39:23:

a) "The skins of those who fear their Lord tremble thereat … then their skins and their hearts do soften to the celebration of Allah's praises. Such is the guidance of Allah: He guides therewith whom He pleases, but such as Allah leaves to stray, can have none to guide."

b) HQ 45:11 "This (Quran) is a true Guidance …"

c) HQ13:2-3 "… He (God) regulates all affairs, explaining the signs in detail, that ye may believe with certainty in the meeting with your Lord". Certainty will be for those who consider and understand.

d) HQ19:76 "And God doth advance in guidance those who seek guidance …"

e) HQ 75:17 and 19 "It is for Us to collect it and promulgate it. Nay, more, it is for Us to explain it."

The revelation of the Quran has step-by-step confirmed the law of Moses and the Gospel of Jesus. It is a guide from God, and appeals to reason and understanding. Let us understand it rightly in reverence and truth, unswayed by those who reject Faith, and seeking ever the reward of the pleasures of God, through firmness, patience, discipline and charity, and offering others the light which we have ourselves received.

Have you read and studied the Holy Quran? Read and learn about Islam/Muslim—meaning a person who practices Islam, that is One who surrenders himself to the Will and Purpose of Allah (God).

Are you not frightened that you may be on the wrong path? By studying the Holy Quran, at least you will gain knowledge and wisdom and be sure that you are on the right path that you are now following. Do not be deceived by the illusion of vicarious atonement. Do not be arrogant. My duty is only to remind you that you may learn to fear/love Allah (God).

HQ 23:78 "It is He who has created for you the faculties of hearing, sight, feeling, and understanding: little thanks is it ye give."

Some quotes of what the Quran says of itself:

HQ38:29 "A book which We have sent down unto thee, full of blessing. . ."

HQ 65:11 The Quran is a message – "…containing clear explanations …"

HQ 44:2 The Quran " …makes things clear."

HQ 18:54 "We have explained in detail in this Quran every kind of similitude for the benefit of mankind. But man is in most things contentious."

HQ 5:17. And there hath come to you from God a new light and a perspicuous Book." The Quran is called a 'Perspicuous Book'. The exact translation of the word used in Arabic describing the Quran is 'Mubin'. A simpler word in English, 'plain', may mean unadorned, the opposite of beautiful, and this Book is among the most beautiful, it is the privilege of mankind to read (mind you, in Arabic only). 'Clear' would be right, as far as it means 'unambiguous, self-evident, not involved in mysteries of origin, history, or meaning, one which everyone can understand as to the essentials necessary for him, without the intervention of priests or privileged persons'. The Arabic word 'Mubin' has all these meanings, but it suggests besides, some quality of a shining light, by which we are able to make things clear, to distinguish the true from the false. Therefore, it is suggested that 'perspicuous' would be a better word than 'clear' in describing the Holy Quran.

Besides, it is hardly a good idiom to speak of 'a clear book'.

HQ 8:2-3 Believers are those who:

1. When God is mentioned feel a tremor in their hearts.
2. On hearing His signs rehearsed, find their faith strengthened.
3. Those who put all their trust in their Lord.
4. Who establish regular prayers.
5. Who spend freely out of the gifts of sustenance given to them.

Earlier Books of Revelation had been corrupted by human ignorance, or selfishness or fraud, or misinterpreted altogether.

What other cause would there be for various sects violently disputing with each other as to their true meaning, even to this day?

There are many thousand sects amongst the Christians. See Encyclopedia Britannica, or the information in your computer. Such doubts had to be set to rest, and they were set to rest by the Revelation of the Quran, by inspiration directly from God, Lord of the universe.

The Quran is perfect as God is perfect. The Quran does not consist of human conjecture; nor is it reconstructed philosophy in which there is always room for doubt and dispute. Only God is perfect, therefore aim for perfection in all that you do. You will never reach perfection but you will gain excellence in all that you do.

HQ 5:51 "To thee We send the scripture in truth, confirming the scripture that came before it, and guarding it in safety …". The Holy Quran confirms what was revealed before it and guarded in safety is its original revealed form, without a single mistake/change in meaning/interpretation (in Arabic).

Refer HQ 29:23. "Those who reject the Signs (that is the Holy Quran) of God and the Meeting with Him… will despair of God's Mercy and suffer a grievous Penalty."

Refer HQ 25:32. The Holy Quran was revealed/rehearsed in slow and well-arranged stages to strengthen Prophet Muhammad's heart.

HQ 41:41. "…And indeed it is a Book of exalted power."

HQ 18:1. There is no crookedness in the Quran.

HQ 18:2. It is a straight, clear and perspicuous Quran.

HQ 4:174. "… We have sent unto you a Light that is Manifest."

HQ 20: 99. The Quran is from God. "…We have sent thee a Message from Our Own Presence."

HQ 10:64. "… No change can there be in the Words of God."

HQ 86:13. "Behold this (The Quran) is the Word that distinguishes (Good from Evil)"

HQ 85:21 and 22. "Nay, this is a Glorious Quran, inscribed in a Tablet Preserved".

God's message is not ephemeral. It is eternal.

The Tablet is not to be understood in a material sense, made of stone or metal. It is preserved or guarded from corruption.

HQ 15:9. "We have without doubt, sent down the Message and We will assuredly guard it" (from corruption). For the past 14 centuries, there has not been a single change, in word, singular/plural, or vowels. In the Arabic Quran, God's Holy Truth will never suffer eclipse or corruption even though the whole world was bent on destroying it.

HQ 27:76. "Verily this Quran doth explain to the children of Israel most of the matters in which they disagree."

The Jews had numerous sects. Some were altogether beyond the pale, e.g. the Samaritans, who had a separate Taurat of their own: They hated the other Jews and were hated by them. But even in the orthodox body there were several sects of which the following may be mentioned:

a) The Pharisees, who were literalistic, formalists, and fatalists, and had a large body of traditional literature, with which they overlaid the Law of Moses.

b) The Sadducee, who were rationalists, and seemed to have doubted the doctrine of Resurrection or of a Hereafter.

c) The Essenes, who practiced a sort of Communism and asceticism and prohibited marriage. About many of the doctrines they had bitter disputes, which were settled by the Quran, which supplemented and perfected the Law of Moses. It also explained clearly the nature of God and of Revelation, and the Doctrine of the Hereafter.

HQ 29:46. The Quran tells us Muslims not to dispute with "the people of the book" that is, Jews and Christians "except with means better." With kindness, sincerity, truth and genuine anxiety for the good of the reader without seeking selfish or questionable aims. Finally leaving to his God-given reason all that is in The Book of the Universal Religion.

HQ 41:2,3 and 4. The Quran is:

1. A Revelation from Allah.
2. A Book wherein the verses are explained in detail.
3. A Quran in Arabic (the language of the people among whom it was first promulgated) for people who understand.
4. Giving Good news and Admonition.
5. However, most turn away and hear not.
6. HQ 31:3. "This Quran is certainly a guide and a mercy to the Doers of Good."
7. HQ 41:42. "No falsehood can approach it from before or behind it ... i.e. God's Truth is fully guarded on all sides. No one can get the better of it by attacking it from before or behind it, openly or secretly, or in any way whatsoever.
8. HQ16:89 It is "The Book explaining all things, a Guide, a Mercy, and Glad Tidings to those who have surrendered to the Will and Purpose of God" i.e. Muslims.
9. HQ 7:52 "A Guide and a Mercy to all who believe."
10. HQ 6:38 "Nothing has been omitted from the Quran."
11. HQ 10:37. "This Quran is not such as can be produced by other than God."

12. It is a confirmation of revelations that came before it and gives a fuller/clearer explanation of the earlier Revelations of the Book wherein there is no doubt from the Lord of the Worlds. 'The Book' here means all the revelations sent to earlier Messengers and Prophets, essentially the Same Message.
13. HQ 32:2. "This is the revelation of the Book in which there is no doubt, from the Lord of the Worlds."
14. HQ 49:21. "Had We sent down this Quran on a mountain, verily thou would have seen it humble itself and cleave asunder for fear of God. Such are the similitudes which We propound to men, that they may Reflect".

God's revelation through the ages is one. The Quran confirms, fulfils, completes and further explains the One True Revelation, which has been sent by the One True God in all ages.

The Quran not only gives us rules for our everyday conduct, but speaks of high matters of mystic significance, which require elucidation in three ways, namely:

a) By instruction from Teachers of great spiritual experience.
b) By experience from actual facts of life.
c) By the final fulfilment of the hopes and the warnings which we now take on trust through our faith. My dear reader if you reject God's Message simply because you cannot understand it, without even giving it a chance of elucidation in any of the above given three ways, then "to you be your way and to me mine" HQ 109:6.

Muslims having been given the Truth, cannot come to false ways of men with vested interests. For them the responsibility is theirs. The Truth must prevail in the end. This was the attitude of Faith then: but it is true for all time. Hold fast to Truth, in scorn of consequences.

The Quran is meaningful and good for all time, past, present, and future. All statements hold good for the present as they are workable and practical in our time, and will hold good for the future also. Take any statement and check it out with your reason.

HQ 39:23. "God has revealed the most beautiful Message in the form of a Book consistent with itself yet repeating its teaching in various aspects. The skins of those who fear their Lord tremble thereat."

HQ 74:54. "Nay, this Quran surely is an admonition." HQ 41:43. "The Quran does not relate anything else than what was revealed to all the prophets earlier.

Nothing is said to thee (prophet Muhammad) that was not said to the apostles before thee." The gist is that, 'The Message' to all the prophets now, before and forever is the same; that is, Mercy to the erring and repentant, and just punishment to those who willfully rebel against God.

HQ 69:51. "But verily it (The Quran) is Truth of assured Certainty."

All Truth is in itself certain. But as received by men, and understood with reference to men's psychology, certainty may have degrees. There is the probability or certainty resulting from the application of men's power of judgement and his appeasement of evidence. This is certainty by reasoning or inference. Then there is the certainty of seeing something with our own eyes. Seeing is believing. This is certainty by personal inspection. Then, as here, there is the absolute Truth, with no possibility of error of judgement or error of the eye (which includes any instrument of sense perception and any ancillary aids, such as microscope, telescope, X ray, radar etc. The Absolute Truth is the one spoken of here—that is no possibility of error of judgement, or error of eye or instrument.

HQ 12:103. 'Yet no faith will the greater part of mankind have, however ardently thou dost desire it."

HQ 61:9. "It is He who has sent his Apostle with guidance and the Religion of Truth, that He may proclaim it over all religion, even though the Pagans may detest it"

Note: 'Religion of Truth'—Islam over all religion is mentioned three times in the Quran: HQ 9:33, HQ 48:28, and HQ 61:9. Please note that 'Over all Religion' is in the singular, and not over all other religions (plural). There is really only one True Religion, the Message of God, The Supreme Being. Submission to the Will of God is called Islam. It was the Religion preached by Moses and Jesus (May peace and blessings of Allah be upon them both). It was the religion of Abraham, Noah, and all other prophets, by whatever name it may be called. If people corrupt that pure light, and call their religion by different names, we must bear with them, and we may allow the names for convenience. But Truth must prevail over all.

HQ 39:41. "Verily We have revealed The Book to thee in Truth, for instructing mankind. He then that receives guidance benefits his own soul, but he that strays, injures his own soul ..."

HQ 30:58. "We have put forth for men in this Quran every kind of Parable in order that they may receive admonition."

Men can understand high spiritual truths by parables and similitude, therefore every kind of Parable has been put forth in the Quran not merely to tell stories but to teach lessons of spiritual wisdom, and 'in order that they may receive admonition'. Men should not behave arrogantly against all Truth and Reason.

HQ 31: 1-5. "These are verses of the Wise Book. A Guide and a Mercy to the doers of good, those who establish regular prayers, and give regular charity and have (in their hearts) the assurance of the hereafter. These are on true guidance from their lord; and these are the ones who will prosper."

HQ 2:1-7. "This is the Book, in it is guidance sure without doubt, to those who:

1. Fear Allah/Love Allah so that they fear to do what their conscience tells them is wrong, bad, or evil.
2. Believe in the unseen i.e. Angels.
3. Are steadfast in prayer i.e. Consistent in prayers.
4. Spend out of what We have provided for them. i.e. Charity and Zakath, i.e. 2½% of excess holdings per year.
5. Believe in the revelation sent to thee (Prophet Muhammad)
6. Believe in the revelations sent to prophets before Prophet Muhammad. i.e. all prophets.
7. Have the assurance of the hereafter."

Those who practice these seven points mentioned above—they, and only they, will have True Guidance from their Lord, and it is these who will prosper. The helpless case is that of an obstinate man whose heart is so dead, that he does not advance to the right even though his reason so dictates, nor does he withdraw from the wrong.

HQ 4:82 "Do they not consider the Quran with care? Had it been from other than Allah (God) they would surely have found therein much discrepancy."

One can find much discrepancy in all other religious books.

HQ 54:40 "… and We have indeed made the Quran easy to understand and remember. Then is there any that will receive admonition?"

It is a fact that the Quran with 114 chapters and 6238 verses, is known by heart to millions of Muslims all over the world (many in their teens, or younger). Mind you the

Quran is known and easy to remember only in Arabic — the language in which it was propounded/ promulgated.

HQ 36:69. "… It is a Quran making things clear." HQ 10:1. It is a Book of Wisdom.

HQ 75: 17,18, and19. "It is for Us to collect it and to promulgate it. But when We have promulgated it, follow thou its recital as promulgated."

The Quran is collected, arranged, disseminated/made public and explained (by God).

HQ 56:77-80. "That this is indeed a Quran most honourable, a Book well-guarded which none shall touch but those that are clean. A revelation from the Lord of the Worlds."

Your attention is drawn to momentous issues of the Quran. It is a Revelation described by four characteristics:

1. It is most Honourable, which implies besides the fact that it is worthy of great favour receiving honour, that it confers great favours on those who receive it.
2. It is well-guarded, precious in itself and well preserved in its purity.
3. None but the clean will touch it, i.e. clean in body, mind, thought, intention and soul. Only such can achieve real contact with its full meaning.
4. It is a Revelation from the Lord of the Worlds, and therefore universal for all.

HQ 81:26,28 "Then whither go ye? Verily this is no less than a Message to all the Worlds, with profit to whoever among you wills to go straight."

HQ 18:27 "… and none can change the words." i.e, His Commands, Decrees, and Orders, in fact the whole Quran.

HQ 50:1 "By the Glorious Quran…" 'Glorious' is one of the beautiful appellations of the Quran. Its glory is that of the rising sun: the more it rises on your mental and spiritual horizon, the more you are lost in admiration of its glory. Its meanings are manifest and inexhaustible. The greater your experience the more light your spiritual eye is able to bear. And in that glory is a beauty that none can tell who has not experienced it in his soul. It is in itself proof of the mission of the holy Prophet Muhammad.

HQ 39:1, 40:2, 45:2 The revelation of this Book is from Allah (God), Exalted in Power, full of Wisdom and Knowledge.

HQ 98:7 "Those who have faith and do righteous deeds, they are the best of creatures."

To be given the faculty of discrimination between right and wrong and then to reject truth, is the worst folly which a creature endowed with will can commit. It must necessarily bring its own punishment whether the creature calls himself one of the children of Abraham (or one of the redeemed of Christ Jesus, or whether he goes by the mere light of Nature and reason as a pagan. Honour in the sight of God is not due to race or profession of faith but to sincere and righteous conduct (HQ 49:13).

In the end, one could say that among the beauties of the Quran, not the least is that which sends its mystic interpreters into ecstasies of spiritual delight, while its plain meaning contains noble precepts of ordinary conduct, its mystic passage reveal spiritual mysteries which can only be expressed by the phrase, "Light upon Light." (HQ 24:35). It is an endless chain of illumination in which ordinary knowledge dissolves as if it were ignorance.

Chapter 6

THE HOLY BIBLE

The Christian covenant may be taken as the charge Prophet Jesus gave to his disciples, and which the disciples accepted to welcome Prophet (Muhammad) Ahmed.

See Gospel of St. John as it exists now.

John 15:26 "But when the Helper comes whom shall I send to you from the Father (God), the Spirit of truth, who proceeds from the Father (God), he will testify of Me."

Who is the 'Helper'? It is Prophet Muhammad as he was testified by Prophet Jesus. HQ 61:6. "And remember, Jesus the son of Mary, said: 'O children of Israel! I am the apostle of God sent to you, confirming the Law which came before me, and giving glad tidings of an Apostle to come after me, whose name shall be Ahmed…' "

John 16:13 "However, when He the Spirit of truth has come He will guide you unto All Truth: (Mind you, not just Truth, but All Truth) for He will not speak on His own authority, but whatsoever He hears He will speak: and He will tell you things to come."

Prophet Muhammad was unlearned (Refer HQ 7:157 and 62:2). He recited the Holy Quran as told to him by Angel Gabriel.

HQ 5:75 "They do blaspheme who say God is Christ the son of Mary…" Compare the Bible Matt. 4;10, where Jesus Christ rebukes Satan desiring the worship of other than God; John 20:17 Where Jesus Christ says to Mary Magdalene, "Go unto my brethren, and say unto them, I ascend unto my Father and your Father; and to my God and your God." Compare also Luke 18:19, where Jesus rebukes a certain ruler for calling him 'good master'. "Why callest thou me good? None is good, save one, that is God." In Mark 12:29, Jesus Christ says "The first of all commandments is 'Hear, O Israel, the Lord our God is one Lord.'"

All the above quotes are from the Red Letter Bible — meaning all that Jesus Christ has said himself, and not what the Nicea Council has stated, nor what has been written by Mathew, Mark, Luke and John about Jesus Christ long after he was dead/crucified/ascended into Heaven, whatever each one of you readers believe. If one calls himself a Christian, then he has to follow what Jesus Christ has said and not what others proclaim or say about him.

Jewish and Christian Scriptures, as they stand, cannot be traced direct to Moses or Jesus, but are later compilations. Modern scholarship and higher criticism has left no doubt on the subject.

See appendix 1 and 2 on Jewish Scripture and the Bible.

HQ 61:6 "And remember, Jesus the son of Mary, said "O Children of Israel! I am the apostle of Allah (God) sent to you, confirming the Law which came before me, and giving glad tidings of an apostle to come after me whose name shall be, Ahmed. But when he came to them with Clear Signs, they said this is evident sorcery". Original saying of Jesus Matt. 12:31-32, wherein Jesus gives a warning:

31 "Therefore I say to you, every sin and blasphemy will be forgiven men, but the blasphemy against the Spirit (God) will not be forgiven men." Doesn't your reason say that it is obvious Jesus is not God?

32 "Any one who speaks a word against the son of Man (Jesus) it will be forgiven him; but whoever speaks

against the Holy Spirit (God), it will not be forgiven him, either in this age or in the age to come."

HQ 39:32. "Who then doth more wrong than one who utters a lie concerning God, and rejects the Truth when it comes to him…?

Mark 13:32. No one knows the Day or the Hour. "But of that day and hour no one knows neither the angels in heaven, nor the son, but only the Father." A question, only the Father knows, son does not know, if son is God then he, Jesus, must know.

(1) St. John 14:16. "And I will pray the Father, and He shall give you another Comforter, that he may abide with you forever."

a) Who is 'I' in the above verse? By reason, it has to be Jesus.

b) Who is Father? Reason again denotes it is God.

c) Who is 'Another Comforter? Again reason denotes it to be Prophet Muhammad.

St. John 15:26 states "But when the Comforter is come, whom I will send unto you from the Father, the Spirit of Truth, who proceedeth from the Father, he will testify of me."

Only Prophet Muhammad has testified Jesus in the Holy Quran. The Holy Quran has the name of Jesus mentioned seventy eight times and the name of Prophet Muhammad four times (HQ 47:2).

(2) A Warning: St. Matt. 12:31 and 32. "Whoever speaketh against Jesus (son of Mary) it shall be forgiven him, but whoever speaketh against the Holy Spirit, it shall not be forgiven him, neither in this world, nor in the world to come."

And verse 32 reads: "Wherefore I say unto you, all manner of sin and blasphemy shall be forgiven unto men, but the blasphemy against the Holy Spirit shall not be forgiven unto men." Reason dictates that the 'Holy Spirit' is God, and 'son of man' and men, here refers to Jesus, and other prophets and teachers.

The words of 2 Timothy 3:15-17 are very straight-forward and true and good: "All scripture is given by inspiration of God, and is profitable for:

1. Doctrine,
2. Reproof,
3. Correction, and
4. Instruction in Righteousness, that man of God may be complete, thoroughly equipped for every good work."

It is very reasonable to categorize God's word in the above four headings:

a) Genesis 38:13-18. Son of Judah, Er, was wicked, so God killed him — Moral category 2, Reproof.
b) Son of Judah, Onan — selfish envy, so God slew him. — Again, moral category 2, Reproof.
c) Perez and Zerah. Predecessors of the only begotten son of God. — Moral. Nil. Only Incest.

In this regard, we tell our children anecdotes and fables like 'Fox and the Grapes', 'The Wolf and the Lamb', 'The Dog and his shadow' etc. The moral here – not to be greedy. However, in Genesis 19:30-36, 35:15- 18 and 22, 38:13-18, the moral is nil, as these verses refer to Incest.

The daughters of Lot deliver a son each who became famous in the Bible as the progenitors of the Ammonites and the Moabites—the specially guarded and protected communities. What is the moral, or lesson to be learned from the shameless lewd story? Why did God not reproach Lot or strike him with punishment like AIDS, instead of giving his offspring a blessed race? All this is immoral.

Similarly, what is the moral/lesson /reproof/ correction / or instruction in righteousness of the following?

1. 2 Samuels 13:5, 16: 21:23
2. Ezekiel 16:33-34, 23: 1-35
3. Proverbs 7:7-22
4. Song of Solomon 1:12-13, 3:1-4, 4:1-7
5. Judges 16:1
6. Leviticus 18: 8-18

The above quotes are not printed to keep this book clean. The Bible may be referred to.

Do you, dear reader, consider the Bible as Allah's (God's) revelation? Then why do so many mistakes/ contradictions exist in the Bible? God is perfect. He cannot make mistakes. Yes, we do consider that the Bible was written by human beings—Saints Mathew, Mark, Luke, and John—and that they are not perfect and can make mistakes. Reason dictates that this is a fact and has to be accepted. This being so, God has sent another Revelation through Angel Gabriel to Prophet Muhammad in which you will find no mistakes/ contradictions/or whatever else you may decide to find fault with; namely, The Holy Quran, only in Arabic.

HQ 39:32. "Who then doth more wrong than one who utters a lie concerning God, and rejects the Truth when it comes to him: Is there not in Hell an abode for blasphemers?" When man deliberately adopts and utters falsehoods against his own creator, in spite of the Truth being brought, as it were, to his very door by God's signs, what offence can we imagine more heinous than this? To drive home the point of blasphemy and a dire warning, once again read Matt. 12:31-32. In Christian theology this is a blasphemy 'against the Holy Spirit'. "Whosoever speaketh a word against the son of man (Jesus), it shall be forgiven him, but whosoever speaketh against the Holy Spirit (God), it shall not be forgiven him, neither in this world, neither in the world to come."

HQ 5:75. "They do blaspheme who say 'God is Christ the son of Mary'. But said Christ 'O Children of Israel! Worship God my Lord and your Lord'. Whoever joins other gods with God, God will forbid him the Garden and the Fire will be his bode. There will for the wrongdoers be no one to help."

HQ 5:76. "They do blaspheme who say: God is one of three in a Trinity: for there is no god except One God. If they desist not from their word (of blasphemy), verily a grievous penalty will befall the blasphemers among them."

Please refer to the Holy Bible (Matt. 4:10), where Christ rebukes Satan for desiring the worship of other than God; John 20:17, where Jesus says to Mary Magdalene, "… go unto my brethren, and say unto them, I ascend unto my Father and your Father; and to my God and to your God." Refer also to Luke `18:19 where Jesus rebukes a certain ruler for calling him a 'Good Master'. "Why callest thou me good? None is good, save One; that is, God." In Mark 12:29, Jesus says "The first of all commandments is, Hear O Israel; the Lord our God is one."

Man has a spiritual obligation under an implied Covenant with God. God has given man reason, judgement, the higher faculties of the soul, and even the position of God's Vice-regent on earth, and man is bound to serve God faithfully and obey His will. That obedience begins with cleanliness, in bodily functions, food etc. It goes on to cleanliness of mind and thought, and culminates in purity of motives in the utmost recesses of his heart and soul.

The Athanasian Creed pertains to Athanasius of Alexandria, champion of the doctrine of the Trinity in the Arian controversy. This is a creed, the symbol of doctrine named after Athanasius and formally ascribed to him as its author, but now assigned to a later date, sometimes called the 'Quincunque Vult' meaning 'whomsoever wishes', a

Christian statement of belief focused on Trinitarian doctrine from the first words of Bishop of Alexandria and lifelong opponent of Arianism — Arius, Priest of Alexandria (C250-C366), who denied the true divinity of Jesus.

Chapter 7

SIMILARITIES IN THE BIBLE AND THE QURAN

Oneness of God

(A) Bible: Isaiah 45:5 and 6 "I am the Lord, and there is no other, there is no god besides Me. I will gird you, though you have not known Me, that they may know from the rising of the sun to its setting that there is none besides Me. I am the Lord, and there is none other."

How come Christians include Jesus, Son of Mary— thus contradicting this statement?

HQ 112: 1-4. "Say He is God the One and Only, God the Eternal, Absolute; He Begetteth not, nor is He begotten; and there is none like unto Him."

Forbidden Food

(B) Lev. 11:7,8 "And the swine though it divides the hoof, having cloven hooves, yet, does not chew the cud, is unclean to you. Their flesh you shall not eat. And their carcasses you shall not touch. They are unclean to you."
HQ 5:4 and 2:173 "Forbidden to you (for food) are dead meat, blood, the flesh of swine, and that on which hath been invoked the name of other than God …"

(C) Leviticus 17:13 "… any animal or bird that may be eaten, he shall pour out its blood and cover it with dust." Hence Zubah; or the method of sacrificing an animal or bird in Islam. That is similar to the Jewish practice of kosher meat.

(D) Deut. 4:35 "To you it was shown, that you might know that the Lord Himself is God: there is none other besides Him."

Deut. 6:4 "Hear, O Israel: The Lord our God, the Lord is one."

St. Mathew 4:10 "Then said Jesus to him: 'Away with you, Satan! For it is written you shall worship the Lord your God, and Him only you shall serve.'"

Isaiah 45:5,6 "I am the Lord, and there is no other: there is no god besides Me. . ." 45:6. ". . . that they may know from the rising of the sun to its setting that there is none besides Me. I am the Lord, and there is no other."

Mark 12:28. One of the scribes asked Jesus 'Which is the first commandment of all?' Mark 12:29. "Jesus answered him, 'The first of all the commandments is: Hear, O Israel, the Lord our God, the Lord is One.'"

HQ 43:64. Wherein Jesus says "For God, He is my Lord and your Lord: so worship ye Him: this is a straight way."

HQ 112: 1 to 4 "Say He is God the One and Only, God, the Eternal, Absolute; He begets not, nor is he begotten; and there is none like unto Him."

The usual trick of the ungodly is to refuse to face the Truth. If they are cornered in an argument, they deny what is obvious to reasonable men, and turn their backs. HQ 2:216 "… but it is possible that ye dislike a thing which is good for you and that ye love a thing that is bad for you…"

All mankind is One Brotherhood. Men began to trade on the names of the Prophets and cut off that unity and made sects, and each sect rejoiced in its own narrow doctrine, instead of taking the universal teaching of Unity from God. But this sectarian confusion is of man's making.

It will last for a time, but the rays of Truth and Unity will finally dissipate it.

Read 1 Samuel 2:2, Isiah 44:6,45:5,45:6,45:18; all these verses state only one thing, that God is the One and Only.

Refer John 20:17. Jesus tells Mary Magdalene, "Touch me not, for I am not yet ascended to my Father (i.e. I am not dead yet.) but go to my brethren and say unto them: 'I ascend unto my Father, and your Father and to my God and your God.'"

Bible Luke 18:19. Jesus said unto St. Luke: "Why callest thou Me good? None is good, save One that is God."

St. Mathew 26:39. Jesus prayed: "O my Father, if it be possible, let this cup pass from me; nevertheless, not as I will, but as You will." Who is 'Thou' in the text? It has to be God. Let your reason decide. So, how can Jesus be God or one in three once again? Reason for yourself. Many times Jesus says that whatever he speaks is only that which the Father has told him (Bible: John 12:49 and 50). 'Father' in the text would be similar to the Arabic 'Rab'—meaning sustainer and cherisher, not begetter or progenitor. Similarly, see Acts 3:20 and 21. "... which God has spoken through the mouths of all his holy prophets since the world began."

Chapter 8

PROPHET JESUS

What the Quran says about Jesus Christ:

HQ 5:75. "They do blaspheme who say 'God is Christ the son of Mary' but, said Christ: 'O children of Israel! Worship God, my Lord and your Lord. Whoever joins other gods — God will forbid him the Garden, and the Fire will be his abode. There will for the wrongdoers be no one to help.'"

HQ 5:76. "They do blaspheme who say: God is one of three in a Trinity: for there is no god except One God. If they desist not from their word (of blasphemy), verily a grievous penalty will befall the blasphemers among them."

HQ 5:78. "Christ, the son of Mary, was no more than an Apostle; many were the apostles that passed away before him. His mother was a woman of truth. They had both to eat their (daily) food. See how God doth make his Signs clear to them; yet see in what ways they are deluded away from the truth."

HQ 5:113. "Then will God say 'O Jesus the son of Mary recount My favour to thee and to thy mother. Behold! I strengthened thee with the holy spirit, so that thou didst speak to the people in childhood and in maturity. Behold! I taught thee the Book and Wisdom, the Law and the Gospel. And behold! Thou makest out of clay, as it were, the figure of a bird by My leave, and thou breathest into it, and it becomes a bird by My leave. And thou healest those, born blind and the lepers, by My leave. And behold! Thou bringest forth the dead by My leave … And the unbelievers among them said 'This is nothing but evident magic."'

HQ 19:16 to 22. "Relate in the Book the story of Mary, when she withdrew from her family to a place in the East. She placed a screen to shield herself from them; then We sent to her Our angel and he appeared before her as a man in all respects. She said, 'I seek refuge from thee to God Most Gracious; come not near if thou dost fear God'. He said: 'Nay, I am only a messenger from thy Lord to announce to thee the gift of a holy son'. She said: 'How shall I have a son, seeing that no man has touched me and I am not unchaste?' He said: 'So it will be. Thy Lord saith, 'That is easy for Me: and We wish to appoint him as a sign unto men and a Mercy from Us' it is a matter so decreed.' So she conceived him, and she retired with him to a remote place."

As per the Quran, this is what Jesus said:

HQ 61:6. "And remember, Jesus, the son of Mary said 'O! Children of Israel! I am the apostle of God (sent) to you, confirming the Law (which came) before me and giving glad tidings of an Apostle to come after me, whose name shall be Ahmed.[3] But when he came to them with clear signs they said, ' This is evident sorcery'" In John 16:7, the future comforter cannot be the Holy Spirit as understood by Christians, because the Holy Spirit was already present and helping and guiding Jesus.

---

[3] 1. Ahmed, or Muhammad, which means 'the praised one', is almost a translation of the Greek word 'Periclytos'. In the present Gospel of John 14:16, 15:26 and 16:7 the word used for the apostle is 'comforter'. Comforter in Greek is 'Paracletos' which means Advocate i.e. One called to the help of another, a kind friend, rather than 'Comforter'. Our Muslim scholars contend that Paracletos is a corrupt reading for Pericleytos and that in the original saying of Jesus there was a prophecy of our Prophet Muhammad by name. Even if we read it as Paraclete, it would apply to the Holy Prophet, who is a "Mercy for all creatures" (HQ 21:107) "and Most Kind and Merciful to the Believers." (HQ 9:128).

Compare Matt 4:10, where Jesus rebukes Satan for desiring the worship of other than God.

John 20:17, wherein Jesus says to Mary Magdalene. "… go unto my brethren and say unto them, I ascend unto my Father and your Father, and to my God and your God."

Mark 12:29. Jesus says "The first of all commandments is: Hear, O Israel, the Lord our God is One Lord."

Luke 18:19.wherein Jesus rebukes a certain ruler for calling him 'good master', "Why callest thou me good? None is good save One that is God."

John 15:26. "But when the Helper comes, whom I shall send to you from the Father ie God, the spirit of Truth who proceeds from the Father, i.e. God. He will testify of me."

H.Q 4:171, wherein Jesus is testified by Prophet Muhammad "… Christ Jesus the son of Mary was no more than an Apostle of God and His word …"

HQ 19:30. Jesus in his childhood says: "I am indeed a servant of God. He hath given me revelation and made me a prophet, and He hath made me blessed wheresoever I be and hath enjoined on me Prayer and Charity as long as I live. He hath made me kind to my mother and not overbearing or miserable. So peace be on me the day I was born and the day that I shall die and the day that I shall be raised up to life (again)!"

God has made a Universal software Program. Therefore, you never say anything or behave/act the way you do other than through the Universal Program set by God. All our sayings, thoughts, beliefs, acts are conditioned by this Universal Program.

This is also the teaching of Jesus as reported in the Gospel of St John 12:49,50. "For I have not spoken on my own authority, but the Father who sent me and gave me a Command what I should say and what I should speak. And

I know that His command is everlasting life. Therefore whenever I speak, just as the Father has told me, so I speak."

'Father' herein would mean Creator, Sustainer, and Cherisher, not begetter or progenitor. If Jesus is God, then he would have or, should have said: 'For I speak…'. Refer Matt. 12:31,32 wherein Jesus says: "Wherefore I say unto you: 'all manner of sin and blasphemy shall be forgiven unto men, but the blasphemy against the Spirit will not be forgiven men." Here, 'Spirit' by reason would be God and not Jesus himself.

Next, in verse 32, there is a warning: "And whosoever speaketh a word against the son of man, it shall be forgiven him; but whosoever speaketh against the Holy Spirit (God), it will not be forgiven him, neither in this world, nor in the world to come."

HQ 4:48 says the same thing. "God forgiveth not that partners should be set up with Him; but He forgiveth anything else, to whom He pleaseth; to set up partners with God is to devise a sin most heinous indeed."

Just as in an earthly kingdom the worst crime is that of treason as it cuts at the very existence of the state, so in the spiritual kingdom, the unforgivable sin is that of contumacious treason against God, by putting up God's creatures in rivalry against Him. This is rebellion against the essence and source of spiritual life in what Plato would call 'the lie in the soul'. But even here, if the rebellion is through ignorance, and is followed by sincere repentance and amendment, God's Mercy is always open.

H.Q 4:17. "God accepts the repentance of those who do evil in ignorance and repent soon afterwards; to them will God turn in mercy …"

HQ 3:45,46. "Behold! The angel said: 'O Mary! God giveth thee the glad tidings of a word from Him: his name will be Christ Jesus, the son of Mary, held in honour in this world and the hereafter and (of the company of) those nearest to God. He shall speak to the people in childhood and in maturity, and shall be of the company of the righteous."

The ministry of Jesus lasted about three years, from 30 to 33 years of his age, when in the eyes of his enemies he was crucified. But the Gospel of Luke 2:42 describes him as disputing with the doctors in the temple at the age of 12, Luke 2:47. "And all who heard him were astonished at his understanding and answers. And when Joseph and Mary saw him they were amazed." Luke 2:40; and even earlier as a child, he was "strong in spirit filled with wisdom. And the Grace of God was upon him." Some Apocryphal Gospels describe him as preaching from infancy.

When Mary brought her baby son to her people, the amazement of the people knew no bounds. In any case they were ready to think the worst of her, as she had disappeared from her kin for some time. But now she comes, shamelessly parading her babe in her arms! How she had disgraced the house of Aaron, the foundation of priesthood! We may suppose that the same took place in the temple in Jerusalem, or in Nazareth.

Aaron, the brother of Moses was the first in line of Israelite priesthood. Mary and her cousin Elizabeth (mother of Yaha i.e. John) came of a priestly family, and were therefore Sisters of Aaron or daughters of Imran, who was the father of Aaron. Mary is reminded of her high lineage and the high morals of her father and mother. How, they said, she had fallen and disgraced the name of her progenitors. What could Mary do?

How could she explain? Would they in their censorious mood accept her explanations? All she could do was to point to the child, whom, she knew was no ordinary child. And the child came to her rescue. By a miracle he spoke, defended his mother, and preached – to an unbelieving audience.

HQ 19:88-92. "They say God Most Gracious has begotten a son. Indeed, ye have put forth a thing most monstrous. At it the skies are ready to burst asunder and the mountains to fall down in utter ruin, that they should invoke a son for God Most Gracious. For it is not consonant with the Majesty of God Most Gracious that He should beget a son."

The attribution of a son 'begotten' to God has no basis in fact or in reason. It is only 'word' or 'saying' that issues out of the mouths of those who say "God hath begotten a son", and believe so. It is not even a dogma that is reasoned out, or can be explained in any way that is consistent with the spiritual nature of God.

HQ 12:108. "Say thou (Prophet Muhammad) this is my way. I do invite unto God on evidence clear as the seeing with one's eyes, I and who ever follows me. Glory to God! And never will I join gods with God."

Jesus came to fulfil the Law of the prophets before him, that is the one and only religion. See Matt 5:17. wherein Jesus says "Do not think that I have come to destroy the Law, or the Prophets: I did not come to destroy, but to fulfil."

John. 5:30. Jesus himself said "I can of myself do nothing; as I hear I judge, and my judgement is righteous, because I seek not my own will, but the will of the Father (God) who hath sent me."

HQ 21:26. And they say "God most Gracious has begotten an offspring. Glory to Him. They are (but) servants raised to honour."

HQ 21:27. "They speak not before He speaks and they act in all things by His Command."

In verse 26 above, 'begotten', both to the Trinatrian superstition that God has begotten a son and to the old

Arab superstition that the angels were daughters of God; all such superstitions are derogatory to the Glory of God. The Prophets and the angels are no more than servants of God: they are raised high in honour, and therefore they deserve our highest respect but not our worship.

In verse 27, 'They speak not before' implies that they never say anything before they receive God's command to say it and their acts are similarly conditioned. This is also the teaching of Jesus as reported in the Gospel of St. John 12:49 and 50. "For I have not spoken of myself: but the Father which sent me. He gave me a commandment, what I should say, and what I should speak; and I know that His Commandment is life everlasting: whatever I speak therefore, even as the Father said unto me, so I speak." If rightly understood 'Father' has the same meaning as 'Rab' in Arabic, namely, Sustainer and Cherisher, and not Begetter.

HQ 19:30-35. When Mary brought Baby Jesus to the temple the elders were amazed and implied that she was unchaste. When Mary pointed to Jesus they asked how they could talk to one in a cradle. Then Jesus said, "I am indeed a servant of God: He hath given me Revelation and made me a prophet. And He hath made me blessed wheresoever I be, and hath enjoined on me Prayer and Charity as long as I live. He hath made me kind to my mother, and not overbearing or miserable. So peace is on me the day I was born, the day that I die, and the day that I shall be raised up to life (again). Such was Jesus the son of Mary: (It is) a statement of truth about which they (vainly) dispute.[4]

---

[4] The disputations about the nature of Jesus Christ were not only vain, but also persistent and sanguinary. The modern Christian churches have thrown them into the background, but they would do well to abandon irrational dogmas altogether. Begetting a son is a physical act depending on the needs of man's animal nature. God Most High is independent of

Glory be to Him! When He determines a matter, He only says to it, 'Be', and it is.

What does 'Christ' mean? Christ in Greek (short for Christos) means 'anointed': Kings and priests were anointed to symbolise consecration to their office. The Hebrew and Arabic form is Masiah; in English, Messiah. Therefore, the word Christ is a designation and not a name. Jesus is the right name for the son of Mary, the prophet who was anointed.

The name of Prophet Jesus is mentioned 78 times in the Quran, whereas the name of Prophet Muhammad appears only 4 times.

HQ 4:156. "That they (the Jews) rejected Faith: That they uttered against Mary a grave false charge."

The false charge against Mary was that she was unchaste. Such a charge is bad enough to make against any woman, but to make it against Mary, the mother of Jesus was to bring into ridicule God's power itself.

HQ 4:157. "That they (The Jews) said in boast, 'We killed Christ Jesus the son of Mary, the Apostle of God'

— But they killed him not, nor crucified him, but so it was made to appear to them, and those who differ therein are full of doubts, with no certain knowledge, but only conjecture to follow. For a surety they killed him not."

HQ 4:158. "Nay, God raised him (Jesus) up unto Himself: and God is exalted in Power, Wise."

The end of the life of Jesus on earth is as much involved in mystery as his birth, and indeed the greater part of his private life except the three main years of his ministry. It is not profitable to discuss the many doubts and conjecture among the early Christian sects and among Muslim theologians.

---

all needs, and it is derogatory to Him to attribute such an act to Him. It is merely a relic of pagan and anthropomorphic materialist superstitions.

The Orthodox Christian Churches make it a cardinal point that his life was taken on the cross, that he died and was buried, that on the third day he rose in the body with his wounds intact, and walked about and conversed, and ate with his disciples and was afterwards taken up bodily to Heaven. This is necessary for the theological doctrine of blood sacrifice and vicarious atonement for sins, which is rejected by Islam.

But some of the early Christian sects did not believe that Christ was killed on the Cross. The Basilidans believed that someone else was substituted for him. The Docetae held that Jesus never had a real physical or natural body, but only an apparent or phantom body, and that his crucifixion was only apparent, not real. The Marconite Gospel (about A.D.138) denied that Jesus was born, and merely said that he appeared in human form. The Gospel of St. Barnabas supported the theory of substitution on the Cross. The Quranic teaching is that Jesus was not crucified nor killed by the Jews. All this— the disputations, doubts and conjectures on such matters— is vain.

HQ 4:171 "…Christ Jesus the son of Mary was (no more than) an apostle of God and His Word which He bestowed on Mary, and a Spirit proceeding from Him: So believe in God and His apostles. Say not 'Trinity'. Desist: it will be better for you. For God is one God: Glory be to Him. (Far Exalted is He) above having a son. To Him belong all things in the heavens and on earth. And enough is God as a Disposer of affairs."

HQ 5:113, 114 "Then will (Allah) God say: "O Jesus the son of Mary, Recount My favour to thee and to thy mother. Behold! I strengthened thee with the holy spirit, so that thou did speak to the people in childhood and in maturity. Behold! I taught thee the Book and Wisdom, the Law and the Gospel. And behold! thou makest out of clay, as it were, the figure of a bird, by My leave. And thou breathest into it, and it becometh a bird by My leave, and thou healest those born blind, and the lepers, by My leave. And behold! Thou bringest forth the dead by My leave. And behold I did restrain the Children of Israel from violence to thee when thou didst show them the Clear Signs, and the unbelievers among them said 'this is nothing but evident magic.'"

HQ 5:114 "And behold! I inspired the Disciples to have faith in Me and My Apostle: They said 'we have faith, and do thou (i.e. Jesus) bear witness that we bow to God as Muslims.'"

Before or after Muhammad's life on this earth, all who bowed to God's Will were Muslims, and their religion is Islam.

HQ 4:136 "O ye who believe! Believe in God and his Apostle, and the scripture which he hath sent to His Apostle (Prophet Muhammad) and the scripture (The Red Letter Bible) which He sent to those before him. Any who denieth God, His angels, His Books, His Apostles, and the Day of Judgement, hath gone far astray."

HQ 10:37 "The Quran is not such as can be produced by other than God; on the contrary it is a confirmation of (revelations) that went before it, and a fuller explanation of the Book—wherein there is no doubt—from the Lord of the Worlds".

God's revelation throughout the ages is one. The Quran confirms, fulfils, completes, and further explains the one true revelation, which has been sent by the One True God in all ages.

Chapter 9

PROPHET MUHAMMAD

Michael H. Heart, astrophysicist and amateur historian ranks Prophet Muhammad at the top of the list of the 100 most successful men in the world and invites readers to challenge his selections in his book Hearts 100. Prophet Muhammad is first; the most successful person among the billions born thus far, the founder of Islam. (Actually he just revived Islam. Islam was the only religion prophesied by all the Prophets). He was placed on top of the list of the 100 most successful men in the world based on the following criteria or objective standards for judging greatness:

1. The leader must provide for the well being of the led.
2. The leader or would-be-leader must provide a social organization in which they feel relatively secure.
3. That this leader must provide his people with a set of beliefs. Many bought the book, interested only in reading about the 100 most successful men and the most successful man, rather than in the reasons for their supreme success. There is a general tendency on the part of most men to hero-worship, rather than taking the examples to be followed and set their heroes as role models. Such men find solace in the glorious description of historical personalities. History is often the refuge of those who have done little themselves worth celebrating.

That is foregoing or sacrificing of prestige and ego with patience. Sacrifice of honour is far greater than that of life with war/fighting.

What the Quran says about Prophet Muhammad:

Prophet Muhammad was foretold by Prophet Jesus HQ61:6 wherein Jesus says: "… O children of Israel, I am the Apostle of God sent to you, confirming the law which came before me, and giving glad tidings of an Apostle to come after me, whose name shall be Ahmed (The praised one)…"

See what Jesus says in John 15:26 "But when the helper comes, whom I shall send to you from the Father, the Spirit of Truth who proceeds from the Father, he will testify of me."

In the Quran, Jesus is testified and praised and mentioned 78 times whereas Prophet Muhammad's name is mentioned only 4 times in the Quran.

Further, refer John 16:7, wherein Jesus says "Nevertheless I tell you the truth, it is to your advantage that I go away, for if I do not go away the Helper will not come to you; but if I depart, I will send him to you."

John16:13 "However, when He, the Spirit of Truth, has come, He will guide you into all Truth, for He will not speak on His own authority, but whatever He hears He will speak, and He will tell you things to come."

Prophet Muhammad was sent by God in five capacities. Refer HQ 33:45 and 46:

1. He comes as a Witness.
2. He comes as a bearer of Glad Tidings of the Mercy of God.
3. He comes as a Warner.
4. He comes as one who has the right to invite all men to repentance and the forgiveness of sins, by the permission of God.
5. He comes as a Light or Lamp to illuminate the whole world/universe.

Refer HQ 46:9. Wherein Prophet Muhammad is asked to say "… I am no bringer of new-fangled doctrine among the apostles..." What is there to forge? All prophets have taught the Unity of God, and our duty to mankind. He (Prophet Muhammad) brought no newfangled doctrine, but the Eternal Truths that have been known to good men through the ages.

Prophet Muhammad was granted 5 things which no other Prophet was granted. They are:

1. The whole world as a place of worship and cleansing.
2. Granted permission of intercession i.e. ability to plead for his followers.
3. Given victory against enemies with awe.
4. War booty made lawful to him.
5. Every prophet was sent to his people/nation, but Muhammad was sent to the whole world/universe.

Chapter 10

WHAT THE BIBLE SAYS ABOUT PROPHET MUHAMMAD

What does the Bible say about Prophet Muhammad? There has been a 235% increase in Islam over the past 50 years or so. Islam is the fastest-growing religion; over a billion followers now.

If your answer to the question above is 'nothing', my next question is: how come Prophet Muhammad who is responsible for bringing into being a world- wide community of billion-plus believers who on his authority believe in:

a) The miraculous birth of Jesus
b) That Jesus is the Messiah
c) That Jesus gave life to the dead by Allah's (God's) permission, and that he healed those born blind and the lepers by Allah's (God's) permission.

Surely the Bible must have something to say about this great leader of men who spoke so well of Jesus and his mother Mary?

There are hundreds, nay thousands of prophecies about the coming of Jesus in the Old Testaments. Yes?

If your answer is yes to the above question, then can you give a single prophecy where Jesus is mentioned by name? The words Messiah and Christ are titles (Both the words mean one who is anointed, in Aramic and Greek).

Well, then what are the prophecies of Jesus and Muhammad?

Prophecy. What is it? A word picture. You have to deduce, you have to reason, you have to put two and two together. Therefore, if this is what you do to justify with a thousand prophecies the genuineness of Jesus, then should we not take the same reasoning or adopt the very same system for Prophet Muhammad?

In Deuteronomy 18:15, the words of Prophet Moses are "The Lord thy God will raise up unto thee a Prophet from the midst of thee, of thy brethren, like unto me: unto him ye shall hearken". The word 'me' refers to Moses. Now let us reason out what the similarities between Jesus and Moses:

a) Jesus was a Jew; so was Moses.

b) Jesus was a prophet; so was Moses.

What other commonalities are there? None. Then why not accept other prophets, ten or more like Solomon, Isaiah, Ezekiel, Daniel, Hosea, Joel, Malachi, John the Baptist, etc.? They were all Jews and all prophets. Why only Jesus?

Again read Deut. 18:18. "I (God), will raise them up a prophet from among their brethren like unto thee, and will put My words in his mouth; and he shall speak unto them all that I shall command him."

Note: Deut 18:22 "... When a Prophet speaketh in the name of the Lord…"All 114 chapters of the holy Quran have this seal, "In the Name of Allah the Beneficent the Merciful."

There are three dissimilarities between Prophet Jesus and Moses:

a) As per Christians, Jesus is God; Moses is not God.

b) Jesus died for the sins of the world, but Moses did not have to die for the sins of the world.

c) Jesus went to Hell for three days but Moses did not.

Therefore, by reasoning, Jesus is not like Moses.

Now let us consider simple, solid, tangible facts wherein your children would have no difficulty in following the eight irrefutable arguments concerning Prophet Moses, Prophet Muhammad and Prophet Jesus:

1. Moses and Muhammad both had a father and a mother, whereas Jesus had only a mother.

2. Both Moses and Muhammad had a normal/natural birth, whereas Jesus' birth was miraculous. Refer St. Matthew 1:18, and the HQ 3:47, which gives better narration.

3. Both Moses and Muhammad married and had children, whereas Jesus remained a bachelor all his life.

4. Both Moses and Muhammad were accepted as Prophets by their people in their very lifetime. Both were troubled by their own, but in the end both were acknowledged. Whereas Jesus came unto his own, but his own received him not. (John 1:11)

Even today—after more than 2000 years, his people, the Jews, have rejected Jesus. Therefore, Jesus is not like Moses, but Muhammad is like Moses.

5. Both Moses and Muhammad were prophets as well as Kings. Definitions:

a) Prophet: A man who receives Divine revelation for the guidance of man and conveys the same to mankind without addition or deletion.

b) King: A person who has the power of life and death over his people. Whether he wears a crown or not is immaterial. Moses possessed this power. (Numbers 15:36).

Muhammad too had the power of life and death over his people.

Jesus stated "My kingdom is not of this world…" (John 18:36). Jesus claimed a spiritual kingdom only.

6. Both Moses and Muhammad brought new laws for the people.
7. Moses brought the Ten Commandments. Jesus did not bring any new laws or regulations.
8. Moses and Muhammad died natural deaths, but Jesus was violently killed on the cross.
9. Both Moses and Muhammad lie buried on earth. Jesus is in Heaven.

From the above it is quite clear that the prophecy of prophet Moses, refer Deut.18:15 and18. Deut.18:18 refers to Prophet Muhammad.

Read Matt.12:31 and 32. By reasoning it is obvious that Jesus is not Allah (God). The Quran 39:32 asks "Who then doth more wrong then one who utters a lie concerning Allah (God), and rejects the truth when it comes to him? is there not in Hell an abode for blasphemers?"

Refer Deut. 18:19. "And it shall be that whoever will not hear My words, which he (a new prophet like Moses) speaks in My name, I will require it of him."

All 114 chapters of the Quran begin with a seal "In the name of Allah the Beneficent the Merciful". (That is God's name as spoken by Prophet Moses in Deut.18:19) except in Chapter 9. However, chapter HQ 27 has this seal twice; one at the beginning and the second in verse 30 (HQ 27:30), authenticating all 114 chapters are spoken by Prophet Muhammad in the name of Allah.

Prophet Abraham's Prayer. HQ 2:129. "Our Lord, send amongst them an apostle of their own, who shall rehearse Thy Signs to them and instruct them in Scripture and Wisdom and sanctify them: For Thou art the Mighty, the Wise."

How many people in all times and among all nations close their hearts to any extension of knowledge or spiritual influence because of some little fragment which they have got and which they think is the whole of Allah's (God's) Truth? Such an attitude really shows want of faith and is a blasphemous limitation of Allah's (God's) unlimited spiritual gifts to His creation. The more knowledge you have of Islam or any other religion/creed, the better your intelligence is equipped to prove and convince you through reasoning that surrendering to Allah (God), is the basic tenet of any religion. Or that all religions in their original uncorrupted form are the same or vice-versa. Islam, means surrendering yourself (or oneself) to the Will and Purpose of Allah (God). If we only reason this out with intelligence then it would mean that all religions in their pristine form are one and the same. They have to be as One Allah (God) teaching one class, the universe; and the one same subject.

Islam existed before the preaching by Prophet Muhammad on this earth. HQ 3:67 expressly calls prophet Abraham a Muslim. Its teaching — i.e. Submission to Allah's (God's) Will — has been and will be the teaching of religion for all time and to all peoples and intelligent beings, that is, the whole universe.

The Islamic Creed. HQ 2:136 "Say ye: We believe in Allah (God) and the revelation given to us, and to Abraham, Ismail, Isaac, Jacob, and the tribes, and that given to Moses and Jesus, and that given to all the Prophets from their Lord: We make no difference between one and another of them. And we bow to Allah (God) in Islam."

And again HQ 3:84. Say "We believe in Allah (God), and in what has been revealed to us and what was revealed to Abraham, Ismail, Isaac, Jacob, and the tribes, and in the books given to Moses, Jesus, and the prophets, from their Lord: We make no distinction between one and another among them, and to Allah (God) do we bow our will in Islam."

In these two verses of the Quran quoted above, we have the Creed of Islam, to believe in

1. The One Universal Allah (God),
2. The Message delivered by other Teachers in the past, are mentioned in three groups:

a) Abraham, Ismail, Isaac, Jacob, and the tribes: of these, Abraham apparently had a Book and others followed his tradition.[5]

b) Moses and Jesus, who each left a scripture. These scriptures are still extant, though not in their pristine form.

c) Other scriptures, Prophets or Messengers of Allah (God), are not specifically mentioned in HQ 40:78. "We make no difference between any of these. Their Message in essence was One as revealed by Allah (God)", and that is the basis of Islam.

Reason dictates that Christianity as preached by Jesus (Red Letter Bible) is Islam. His preaching was for all people. HQ 21:91 and 92. "We made her (Mary), and her son (Jesus) a sign for all peoples. Verily this brotherhood of yours (Mankind) is a single brotherhood and I am your Lord and Cherisher: therefore, serve Me and no other."

However, the Bible contradicts this statement that Jesus preached only for the Jews.

---

[5] HQ87: 18 and 19. "No book of Abraham has come down to us." But the Old Testament recognises that Abraham was a Prophet (Gen. 20:7). There is a book in Greek, which has been translated by Mr. G. H. Box, The Testament of Abraham (published by the Society for the Promotion of Christian Knowledge; London, 1927). It seems to be a Greek translation of a Hebrew original. The Greek text was probably written in the second Christian century, in Egypt, but in its present form it probably goes back only to the 9th or 10th century. It was popular among the Christians. Possibly the Jewish Midrash also refers to a Testament of Abraham.

Allah's (God's) Message from age to age is always the same, but that its form may and must differ according to the needs and exigencies of the time to suit the habits, customs, knowledge, culture, beliefs, natural surroundings, and the nature of the society, so that they understand, the same revelation/Message of Allah (God).

To understand the Universal Religion, we human beings must have a) Faith, b) Assured Faith, and c) Discover the Real True Religion by deduction and reasoning.

(a) There are signs external to ourselves, which are far beyond our personal experiences; for them we require Faith. There are signs 'for those who believe'. HQ 45:3. "Verily in the heavens and the earth are signs for those who believe."

(b) Signs of our own human body and its functioning and the animals, including all the insect, germs, birds, fishes, etc. For this, we require assured Faith, that is self-confidence (HQ 45:4).

(c) Signs of our daily experiences from external things which affect us and our lives intimately. These are signs/ questions of deduction by those that are wise, that is by reasoning.

HQ 45:5 "And in the alternation of night and day and the fact that Allah (God) sends down sustenance from the sky and revives therewith the earth after its death, and in the change of the winds, are signs for those that are wise."

Chapter 11

UNITY

Ever this light of unity, this mystic light of God's own Will, has shone and shines with undiminished splendour; the names of many messengers are inscribed in the records of many nations and many tongues, and many were the forms in which this message was delivered, according to the needs of the times and the understanding of the people; and manifold were the lives of the Messengers and manifold also was the response of their people; but they were all witness to the One Truth of God's unity, might, grace and love.

As the records of man are imperfect, and the memory of man unstable, the names of many of these messengers are known in one place and not in another, or among one people and not among others; and some of their names may have perished utterly; but their message stands one and indivisible, even though it may have been forgotten, or twisted by ignorance, error, superstition or perversity, or misunderstood in the blinding light of time or tortuous circumstances.

HQ 42:13. "The same religion has He established for you as that which He enjoined on Noah. That which We have sent by inspiration to thee—and that which We enjoined on Abraham, Moses and Jesus. Namely, that ye should remain steadfast in Religion, and make no division therein. To those who worship other things than God, hard is the way to which thou callest them. God chooses unto Himself those whom He pleases (that is by the Universal Computer Program) and guides to Himself those who turn to Him."

God's religion (Islam—Surrendering oneself to God) is the same in essence, whether given, for example, to Prophets Noah, Abraham, Moses, Jesus, and Muhammad, or to all the other prophets whom we know and those who are forgotten.

The source of Unity is the revelation from God. In Islam it is established as an institution, and does not merely remain a vague suggestion.

Faith, Duty, or Religion are not matters to dispute about. The formation of sects is against the very principle of Religion and Unity. What we should strive for is steadfastness in duty and faith and unity among mankind. That is, all religions, uncorrupted, are one and the same.

Unity, unselfishness, love for God and mankind— these things are inconsistent with self-aggrandizement, unjust suppression of our fellow creatures, false worship, and false conduct to our brethren. The Gospel of Unity, though it is in complete accord with the pure pattern after which God made us, is yet hard to those who love self and falsehood. But Grace is free to all and in His wise plan, He will specially select teachers to show the way to humanity, and no one who turns to Him will lack guidance.

HQ 2:213. "Mankind was one single nation and God sent Messengers with glad tidings and warnings and with them He sent the Book of Truth to judge between people in matters wherein they differ, but through selfish contumacy they did differ; But the people of the Book, after the clear Signs came to them, did not differ among themselves, except through selfish countamacy. God by his Grace guided the Believers to the Truth concerning that wherein they differed. For God guides whom He will to a path that is straight."

There are mainly six Christian sects as per a search on the Internet. They are:

1. Independents
2. Protestants
3. Marginals
4. Orthodox
5. Roman Catholics
6. Anglicans

   And there are over 33,000 denominations.[6]

We think of other people as friends and enemies. In Islam, it is only either friends, or potential friends. If you cannot make a man your friend then one must think that you are deficient in your ability to convince him to be your friend. Or you do not have the patience to do so.

Therefore, the mission of Islam is to unite the World in one Religion by:

1. Gospel of Unity: the more sectarianism and division there is in the world, the more the need for this.
2. It must steadfastly pursue its way.
3. It must not be deflected by worldly or political motives.
4. Its Faith must be directly in God and in God's Revelation.
5. It must judge justly between warring factions, as the Religion of Peace and Unity.

The mission of Islam could be further described as:

1. The God whom it preaches is not an exclusive God. He is Lord of the universe to any given person of whatever faith. He is your God as well as mine.

---

[6] World Christian Encyclopedia by Barret Kurian Johnson. Oxford University Press, 2nd Edition 2001.

2. Islam is not a matter of words; it is deeds which decide; each one of us has personal responsibility for his/her own conduct.
3. There is no cause of contention whatsoever when we preach Unity, Truth, and the Hereafter. And lastly,
4. If you have doubts, the final arbiter is God. And His Throne is the goal of Islam.

Chapter 12

TRINITY

For emphasis, HQ 39:32 is quoted here again:

"Who then doth more wrong than one who utters a lie concerning God, and rejects the Truth when it comes to him! Is there not in Hell an abode for blasphemers?" When a person deliberately adopts and utters false hoods against his own Creator, in spite of the Truth being brought, as it were, to his very door by God's signs, what offence can we imagine more heinous than this?

In Christian theology, this is the blasphemy 'against the Holy Spirit' spoken of in Matt. 12: 31-32:

31"Therefore I say to you, every sin & blasphemy against the Spirit of man (God) will not be forgiven men."

32"Anyone who speaks a word against the son of man (Jesus), it will be forgiven him; but whoever speaks against the Holy Spirit (God), it will not be forgiven him, either in this age or in the age to come."

Arius, an early 4th century Alexandrian Presbyter[7] of early 4th century fought hard for the doctrine of Unity. The concept of Trinity was propounded by Athanasius who was born in and later became the Bishop of Alexandria.

The first General Council of the Christian Church–Nicaea (in Bithynia) decided in AD325, against Arius and unitarianism. The controversy raged until AD381, when the

---

[7] 1. In the early Christian Church, one of the several officers managing the affairs of the local church/minister of the second order/ priest.

Council of Constantinople called by emperor Theodosis the Great, confirmed the Nicene Doctrine of Trinity.

Who is a Christian? Reason dictates 'One who follows Jesus Christ'. All Muslims are true Christians as they believe in Jesus Christ the son of Mary, and in what he preached i.e. The Red Letter Bible, and not in what was written about him by Saints Matthew, Mark, Luke and John and others long after Jesus' death/crucifixion/ ascension to heaven.

A person who plays golf is called a golfer. If he works on machines, he is called a mechanic. One who practises medicine and specialises in surgery is called a doctor/surgeon. Thus one who follows the doctrine of Trinity, should be called a 'Trinitarian', or a Nicaea Councilist, or a Theodosist after Theodosis the Great, who confirmed the Nicene doctrine of Trinity. Nowhere in the Bible can one find Jesus ever mentioning the Trinity—Father, Son and the Holy Spirit.

Can anyone point to the least bit of information, or historical fact, or real knowledge on which he can base his life and belief in the Trinity? Ask yourself or your clergy and draw your own conclusions yourself with your God-given reasoning power. "…Yet is each individual in pledge for his deeds." HQ 52:21.

Jesus clearly stated "You shall worship the Lord your God, and Him only you shall serve."

Refer Luke 4:8, Deut. 6:13.

Arius fought hard for the doctrine of Unity, the simple concept of the Eternal God, as against all the hair-splitting and irrational distinctions in the nature and persons of the Godhead, which finally crystalized in the Doctrine of Trinity, propounded and maintained with much personal acrimony by Athanasisus.

He may be counted as the father of Orthodoxy (as now understood in Christianity) as he systematized the Doctrine of the Trinity — 'three in one and one in three'. Up to the 3rd century AD, the Unitarians had been in the majority in the Christian Church, though some metaphysical scholars had started disputes as to the meaning of 'God becoming man'. They discussed Logos or, the Word, the Power of God, whether the Father or the Son were of the same substance, whether the son could be said to have been created by the father, and numerous questions of that kind.

They do interest us now, but they rent the Christian world into many conflicting sects until the mission of our Holy Apostle dissipated the mist and re-established the Doctrine of Unity on a firm and rational basis.

As I have said, the Christian Churches in the East, as well as the Germanic nations which came into the fold, adhered to Unity although not in the pure form which was made clear in the Quran. Even in Western Christianity, as late as AD 496, Christian sovereigns were sophisticated enough to follow the subtle doctrine of the Trinity. The others were brought into line later through political power.

The Christian creed became narrower and narrower, less and less rational, more and more inclined to use earthly weapons to suppress the eternal truth of God.

In AD 415, the Jews were expelled from Alexandria. In the same year and in the same city, the beautiful, modest and eloquent philosopher and mathematician, Hypatia, was murdered—an outrage against both rationalism and intellectual and religious position of women in society. The murder was a particularly brutal one. She was dragged from her chariot in the streets, stripped naked, and suffered slow death in a Christian Church. The worst feature of the crime was the complicity of the Patriarch of Alexandria, who was not only the chief religious dignitary of the Orthodox Church in Egypt, but the de facto repository of political power.

Meanwhile, the native Christian community—the Coptic Church—which had all along clung to the Monophysite doctrine, a corrupt form of unitarianism, was beyond the pale, and its members were held down as a depressed class by their Orthodox brethren. The latter also, basking in official sunshine, collected power and property into their own hands. As Charles Kingsley remarks in 'Hypatia', 'the Egyptian Church ended in chaos, with idolatrous sects persecuting each other for metaphysical propositions which, true or false, were equally heretical in their mouths because they used them as watchwords for division'. The social conditions produced a certain discontent, for which redress came only with the advent (re-emergence) of Islam.

Chapter 13

REASONING AND MORALITY IN MARRIAGE

The natural sexual union between man and woman through which each becomes spiritually whole, has been perceived as a shameful act. Why?

Sex is not a thing to be ashamed of, or to be treated lightly, or to be indulged in to excess. It is as solemn a fact as any in life. It is compared to a farmer's (or) husbandman's tilth. It is a serious affair to him: he sows the seed in order to reap the harvest, but he chooses his own time and method of cultivation. He does not sow out of season nor cultivate in a manner which will injure or exhaust the soil. He is wise and considerate and does not run riot.

Continuing the simile, every kind of mutual consideration is required for human beings; but above all, we must remember that even in these matters there is a spiritual aspect. We must never forget our souls, and that we are answerable to Allah (God).

It was carnal-minded men who invented the Doctrine of Original Sin:

"Behold, I was shapen in iniquity and in sin did my mother conceive me" (Psalm 51:5).

This is entirely repudiated by reasoning and common sense; and also by Islam, in which the office of the father and mother is held in the highest veneration. Every child of pure love is born pure. Celibacy is not necessarily a virtue, and may be a vice.

"Sex is far more important in the lives of men, than in the lives of women." (Dr. Clifford Rose Adams, Penn. State University, USA). According to the doctor, the subconscious factors influencing selection of a mate in order of importance are:

Man: companionship, sex, love, home, family, helpmate, security.

Woman: love, affection and sentiment, security, companionship, home, family and community acceptance, lastly sex.

Psychologists acknowledge that the body of a woman has a far greater attraction for a man than vice versa.

Islam is a religion of moderation. It is the middle path, keeping an equitable balance between extremes. There is no conflict between flesh and the spirit. The desires and urges of the flesh are Allah (God)-willed, and their satisfaction in reasonable and controlled moderation is legitimate.

Sex is a natural instinct, as natural as hunger. The satisfaction of this urge in a legitimate and reasonable manner is in no way incompatible with the highest moral values.

Properly developed sexual glands and effective control of sexual appetite are both necessary for attaining full intellectual power. Islam forbids celibacy. Matrimony is the norm.

Married life affords opportunities for, and helps to attain, a co-ordinated development of personality. It gives opportunities for the cultivation of many social virtues, such as love, sympathy, fellow feeling, charity, a spirit of self-sacrifice and patience. It is in view of this that the Prophet Muhammad has said that whoever marries, perfects half the religion.

Married life brings quietude and satisfaction in life, which are essential for spiritual advancement. "The married state is my way", said Prophet Muhammad.

Extra-marital relations are strictly forbidden in Islam. Similarly, mingling of the sexes, prostitution and concubinage are forbidden too.

Monogamy is the norm but plurality of wives is permitted. Polyandry however is disallowed. Marriage is a social contract, and divorce is provided for. One of the sayings of Prophet Muhammad is: "Of all things permitted by law, divorce is the most hateful".

The treatment of wives by a husband should be strictly equitable. This is a great discipline. Since it is the duty of the man to maintain his wife, he is given superiority over her—he is the final authority in the household.

Marriage is a most intimate communion, and the mystery of sex finds highest fulfilment when intimate spiritual harmony is combined with the physical link. If religion is at all a real influence in life to both parties or to either party, a difference in this vital matter must surely affect the lives of both more profoundly than differences of birth, race, language, or position in life. It is therefore only right that the parties to be married should have the same spiritual outlook.

Note here, that religion is not a mere label or a matter of custom or birth. The two persons may have been born in different religions, but if by their mutual influence, they come to see the Truth in the same way, they must openly accept the same rites and the same social brotherhood. Otherwise, the position will become untenable, individually or socially.

Why is it that Islam allows its men to marry Christian or Jewish girls, but does not allow Muslim girls to marry a Christian or Jew? Would you call this justice?

The answer is: yes, it is just.

The reason why Islam has laid down such a law is that we Muslims do not believe that Jesus was Allah's (God's) son, but we believe, and do regard him—as we regard Prophet Moses and Prophet Abraham, and all the other prophets mentioned in the Bible—as true Prophets of Allah (God); all of them have been sent to mankind in the same way as the last Prophet, Muhammad, was sent. So, if a Jewish or Christian girl marries a Muslim, she may rest assured that none of the Prophets who are holy to her, will ever be spoken of irreverently among her new family; while on the other hand, should a Muslim girl marry a non-Muslim it is certain that he whom she regards as Allah's (God's) Messenger will be abused, and perhaps even by her own children. For do not children usually follow their father's faith? Do you think it would be fair to expose her to such pain and humiliation?

Why polygamy (up to 4 wives) is permitted in Islam:

Islam is the last and final word of Allah (God) ending His series of messages to mankind. It therefore comes with a general law suitable for all times and places, and for the whole of humanity. It did not legislate for the city dweller only, while neglecting the nomad, nor for the cold regions while ignoring the hot ones, nor for one particular period of time, forgetting later times and generations to come.

Islam recognizes the needs and interests of all people, individuals as well as groups. Among human beings, one may find an individual who has a strong desire for children, but whose wife is barren, chronically ill, or has some other problem. Would it not be more considerate towards her and better for him that he marries a second wife who can bear him children, while retaining the first wife with all her rights guaranteed?

Then there may be the case of a man whose desire for sex is strong, while his wife has little desire for it, or she is chronically ill, has long menstrual periods, or the like. If her husband is unable to restrain his sexual urge, should it not be permitted to him to marry a second wife instead of scouting around for girlfriends?

There are also times when women outnumber men, as for example, after wars which often decimate the ranks of men. In such a situation, it is in the interests of society and of women themselves, that they become co-wives to a man instead of spending their entire lives without marriage, deprived of the peace, affection, and protection of marital life and the joy of motherhood for which they naturally yearn with all their hearts, or as instilled by Nature, Allah (God) for them to experience motherhood? Only three possible alternatives exist for such surplus women who are not married as first wives:

1. to pass their whole lives in bitter deprivation.
2. to become sex objects and playthings for lecherous men or,
3. to become co-wives to men who are able to support more than one wife and who will treat them kindly.

Unquestionably, the last alternative should be seen as a correct, healing remedy for this problem, and that is the judgement of Islam. Who is better than Allah (God) in judgement, for a people who have certain faith?

This is the Islamic 'polygamy' which people in the West consider so abhorrent and to which they react with such hostility, while their own men are free to have any number of girlfriends without restriction, and without any legal or moral accountability, either in respect to the woman or to the children she may bear as a result of this irreligious and immoral plurality of extra-marital relationships. Let the two alternatives — plurality of wives or plurality of illicit affairs — be compared, and ask yourself with reason which is the proper course of action, and which of the two groups is correctly guided!

Chapter 14

THE LAST SERMON
BY PROPHET MUHAMMAD

Prophet Muhammad after praising and thanking Allah, said:

"O People, lend me an attentive ear, for I know not whether after this year, I shall be amongst you again. Therefore, listen to what I am saying to you carefully and take these words to those who could not be present here today."

"O People, just as you regard this month, this day, this city as sacred, so regard the life and property of every Muslim as a sacred trust. Return the goods entrusted to you to their rightful owners. Hurt no one so that no one may hurt you. Remember that you will indeed meet your Lord, and that He will indeed reckon your deeds. Allah (God) has forbidden you to take usury (interest), therefore all interest obligation shall henceforth be waived. Your capital, however, is yours to keep. You will neither inflict nor suffer any inequity. Allah (God) has judged that there shall be no interest and that all the interest due to Abbas ibn Abd'al Muttalib (Abbas, son of Abdul Muttalib, Prophet's uncle) shall henceforth be waived."

"Beware of Satan, for the safety of your religion. He has lost all hope that he will ever be able to lead you astray in big things, so beware of following him in small things. O People, it is true that you have certain rights with regard to your women, but they also have rights over you. Remember that you have taken them as your wives only under God's trust and with His permission. If they abide by your right, then to them belongs the right to be fed and clothed in kindness. Do treat your women well and be kind to them for they are your partners and committed helpers. And it is your right that they do not make friends with anyone of whom you do not approve, as well as never to be unchaste."

"O People listen to me in earnest, worship Allah (God), say your five daily prayers, fast during the month of Ramzan, and give your wealth in Zakat. Perform Haj (pilgrimage to the Kabba in Mecca) if you can afford to. All mankind is from Adam and Eve; an Arab has no superiority over a non-Arab, nor a non-Arab any superiority over an Arab; also, white has no superiority over black, nor black any superiority over white, except by piety and good action. Learn that a Muslim is a brother to every other Muslim and that all Muslims constitute one brotherhood. Nothing shall be legitimate to a Muslim which belongs to a fellow Muslim unless it was given freely and willingly. Do not, therefore, do injustice to yourselves."

"Remember, one day you will appear before Allah (God) and answer for your deeds. So beware, do not stray from the path of righteousness after I am gone.

"O People, no prophet or apostle will come after me and no new faith will be born. Reason well, therefore, O People and understand words which I convey to you. I leave behind me two things, the Quran and my example, the Sunnah, and if you follow these you will never go astray."

"All those who listen to me shall pass on my words to others again; and may the last ones understand my words better than those who listen to me directly. Be my witness, O Allah, (God), that I have conveyed Your Message to Your people."

The words 'The Book' as mentioned in many verses of the Quran means the Revelations sent by Allah (God) to all the prophets—thus to all mankind. It is one and the same. It has to be by reason. It is not the intention of the author to prove that the Bible or any version of it, is not the word of God, as it has many mistakes, contradictions and inconsistencies. God is Perfect and cannot make mistakes. Nor can any human being be perfect. A man's goal should be perfection, and in trying to achieve it he will gain excellence. But perfection, never. Again, only God is perfect. The reader is advised to read Ahmed Deedat's book, The Choice (volumes 1 and 2), to see the contradictions, mistakes and proofs therein that the Bible is not the word of God, other than the 'Red Letter Bible'. Only the 'Red Letter Bible', i.e., the words of Jesus and all other prophets is considered as 'The Book' and believed by all Muslims (who are, and have to be, true Christians). True Christians, who believe only in the 'Red Letter Bible'— what only Jesus Christ has said — is the word of God. To bring home the Creed of Islam, it is once again repeated.

HQ 2:136. "Say ye: 'We believe in God, and the revelation given to us, and to Abraham, Isma'il, Isaac, Jacob, and the tribes, and that given to all prophets from their Lord: We make no difference between one and another of them: and we bow to God in Islam.'"

It is hoped that this book, read with reason, becomes a warning to the heedless, a guide to the erring, an assurance to those in doubt, a solace to the suffering, and a hope to those in despair. Amen.

HQ 81:26-29. (26) "Then whither go ye?" (27) "Verily this is no less than a Message to all the Worlds:"

(28) "(With profit) to whoever among you wills to go right." (29) "But ye shall not will except as God wills, the Cherisher of the Worlds."

It has been shown that these are not the words of a mortal, but that 'The Book' is full of divine wisdom; that its teaching is not that of a madman, but sane to the core and in accordance with human needs; that it freely and clearly directs you to the right path and forbids you the path of evil. Why then hesitate? Accept the Divine Grace; repent of your sins; and come to the Higher Life. God is the Cherisher of the Worlds, Lord of Grace and Mercy, and His guidance is open to all who have the will to profit by it. But that will, must be exercised in conformity with God's Will (Verse 29 above). Such conformity is Islam. Verse 28 points to human free will and responsibility; verse 29 to its limitations.

God's Will may be taken as the 'Universal Computer Program' already set by Him.

If there are any to whom the signs from nature, from within their own heart and conscience, and from the voice of revelation, are not enough to convince them, what possible kind of exposition will they accept? Past events and what you see before you point to the unfailing consequences of all you do.

Dear reader, beware, lest you fall into excesses either in doctrine or in formalism. Just as a foolish servant may go wrong by excess zeal for his master, so in religion, people's excesses may lead them to blasphemy or a spirit the very opposite of religion. The Jewish excesses in the doctrine of formalism, racism, exclusiveness, and rejection of Christ Jesus have been denounced in many places. Here the Christian attitude is condemned, which raises Jesus to an equality with God; in some cases, venerates Mary the mother of Jesus, almost to idolatory; attributes a physical son to God; and invents the doctrine of the Trinity, opposed to all reason. According to Athanasian Creed, unless a man believes in it, he is doomed to hell forever. May the Muslims also beware lest they fall into excesses either in doctrine or formalism.

What happened to all the humans who died before Jesus was born? They were not baptized. Did all of them go to hell? Surely God the Cherisher of all human beings would not have willed so.

Chapter 15

CONCLUSION

In symbolic language, a new entrant into the Palace of Divine Knowledge may yet carry in his mind many of the illusions of the lower world. The transparent crystal of Truth he may yet mistake for the unstable water of worldly vanity, which soils the vestments of those who paddle in it. This leads to many undignified positions and mistakes. But a gentle reader points out the truth. Instead of resenting it, the new entrant is grateful and acknowledges his own mistakes freely and frankly and heartily joins with the teacher in the worship of God, the source of truth and knowledge.

The law of righteousness and Godliness is not a new law, nor are the vanity and short duration of this world preached here for the first time. But spiritual truths have to be renewed and reiterated again and again.

If you misuse God's gifts in intelligence, sight, speech, touch, smell, taste, hearing, reasoning etc. or ignore them, i.e. fail to acknowledge either in word, thought, or in your conduct, that is equivalent to ingratitude or refusal to profit by God's infinite Grace.

All those who revert to Islam, on reading this book, should count not their Islam as a favour upon the author. Nay, God has conferred a favour upon you that "…He has guided you to the Faith, if ye be true and sincere." (HQ 49:17).

A man's actual personal religion depends upon many things — his personal psychology, the background of his life, his hidden or repressed feelings, tendencies, or history (which psychoanalysis tries to unravel) or his hereditary disposition or antipathy, and all the subtle influences of his education and his environment. The tasks before the man of God are:

1. to use any of these which can serve higher ends
2. to purify such as have been misused
3. to introduce new ideas and modes of looking at things
4. to combat what is wrong and cannot be mended.

All for the purpose of leading to the Truth and gradually letting in spiritual light where there was darkness before. If that is not done with discretion and the skill of a spiritual teacher, there may not only be a reaction of obstinacy, but an unseemly show of dishonour to the true God (Allah) and His Truth, and doubts would spread among the weaker brethren whose faith is shallow and infirm. What happens to individuals is true collectively of nations or groups of people. Some think that their own ideas are right. God in His infinite compassion bears with them, and asks those who have pure ideas of faith not to vilify the weakness of their neighbours lest the neighbours in turn vilify the real Truth and make matters even worse than before. Insofar as there are mistakes, God will forgive and send His grace for helping ignorance and folly. Where there is active evil, He will deal with it in His own way. Of course, the righteous man must not hide his light under a bushel, or compromise with evil or refuse to establish right living where he has the power to do so.

Universal acceptance is only for something that has scientific or rational basis. Without scientific support or rational basis, a claim loses validity and is deemed invalid. Today a person is free to follow whatever he wishes in the matter of belief. To get acceptance however, he has to provide scientific support or reasoning for it.

The Quran—and indeed, every religious book—has to be read, not only with the tongue and voice and eyes, but with the truest and purest light which our reason, head and conscience can give us. It is in this spirit that I would have my readers approach the Quran.

Those who are not responsive to realities of the spiritual world are no better than those who are dead. The Message of God penetrates the hearts of those who are alive in the spiritual sense.

It is the nature of sin to be hostile to Truth and Righteousness, but such hostility will not harm the righteous and brook no misgivings because God will guide and help those who work in His cause. And what could be better or more effective than His guidance and help?

It may be noted that before or after Prophet Muhammad's life on this earth, all who bowed to God's Will or resigned to His Will were or are Muslims (those submit to the will of God). As all things and beings proceed from God, so will they return to Him, and He is ever True. Why then does ungrateful man make untrue phantoms for himself instead of rejoicing in the good news which God sends?

Men but wrong their own souls in shutting out the Truth of God. To Him will be their return. They have been warned at all times, among all peoples by chosen Apostles of God whom they have flouted. The Day will come when they will see the Majesty, the Glory, the goodness and the Justice of God. The unbelievers invent fancies and falsehoods. Let not their blasphemies grieve the men of God, for falsehood and false ones will never prosper.

Your trust should be in God, rather than in human pursuits, institutions, or precautions, however good and reasonable they might be.

HQ 5:4 "…This day have I perfected your religion for you, completed My favour upon you, and have chosen for you Islam as your religion."

This is a clear testimony to the perfection of religion in Islam. No such claim is made by any other book or religion. Religion being perfected, no prophet was needed after Prophet Muhammad. HQ 45:14 tells us Muslims "…to forgive those who do not look forward to the Days of God…"; It is for Him to recompense (for good or ill) each people according to what they have earned.

Do not be arrogant against God but come to Him in submission.

One who does not reason is a fool. One who will not, is a bigot, and the one who dares not, is a slave. Most human beings have an almost infinite capacity to take things for granted. Against logic there is no armour like ignorance. So dear reader, I urge you again to reason for yourself.

Those who listen to the truth sincerely and earnestly, they must believe; even if the spiritual faculty is dead, God will by His grace revive it and they will come to Him, if they really try earnestly to understand. The sincere will believe; but those whose hearts are dead will not listen, yet they cannot escape being brought to the Judgement Seat before God.

HQ 12:103 "Yet no faith will the greater part of mankind have, however ardently thou dost desire it."

Even if people profess a nominal faith in God they corrupt it by believing in other things as if they were God's partner, or had some share in the shaping of the world's destinies! For some it is idolatry, the worship of stock and stones. In others it is Christolatory and Mariolatory, or the deification of heroes and men of renown. In others it is the power of nature or of life, or of the human intellect personified in science or arts or inventions, and this is the more common form of modern idolatry.

Others again worship mystery, or imaginary powers of good or even evil: greed and fear are mixed with these forms of worship. Islam calls us to worship the one true God, and Him only.

Islam holds fast to the one central fact in the spiritual world—the unity of God, and all reality springing from Him and Him alone. There can be no one and nothing in competition with that One and only reality. It is the essence of Truth. All other ideas or existences, including our perception of self, are merely relative—mere projections from the wonderful faculties which He has given to us.

This is not, to us, mere hypothesis, it is our inmost experience. In the physical world they say that seeing is believing. In our inner world, this sense of God is as clear as sight in the physical world. Therefore, Muhammad Mustafa and those who really follow him in the truest sense of the word, call all the world to see this Truth, feel this experience, follow this Way. They will never be distracted by metaphysical speculations, whose validity will always be doubtful, nor be deluded by phantoms which lead men astray.

HQ 39:9: "…It is those who are endowed with understanding that receive admonition."Therefore, only men of understanding take heed.

The highest kind of charity is to teach God's given art, skill, or talent, or share with others the product of your skills. As God knows our inner most being, it is absurd for us to justify ourselves either by pretending that we are better than we are, or by finding excuses for our conduct. We must offer ourselves unreservedly, such as we are; it is His Mercy and Grace that will cleanse us. If we try, out of love for Him, to guard against evil, our striving is all that He asks for.

HQ 5:62. "O people of the Book (Christians and Jews) do you disapprove of us (Muslims) for no other reason than that we believe in God and the revelation that has come to us and that which came before us? (That is, to Prophet Moses and Prophet Jesus, and all other prophets before them and perhaps that most of you are rebellious and disobedient.

Perhaps this treatment meted out by God as mentioned in Deut. 11:28 and 28: 15-68: Who were the people who incurred the curse of God? Who provoked God's wrath? See Deut. 1:34 and Matt. 3:7: Who forsook God and worshipped evil? See Jeremiah 16:11-13. That has been the record of past Christians and Jews, and of some even now.

Not for the first nor for the last time, do the righteous suffer plausibly for the guilt of the guilty. HQ 73:19 says: "Verily this is an admonition, therefore, who so will, let him take a straight path to his Lord." Either by adversity or by affluence, God's test will search out our true mettle and reject the dross.

Refer HQ 45:6: If there are any to whom the signs from nature, or from within their own heart and conscience, from the voice of Revelation, are not enough to convince them, what possible kind of exposition will they accept? HQ 21:10 says "We have revealed for you, O men! a book in which is a message for you: Will ye then not understand?"

So, what is the message you have received? The message I received (as perceived by me), was to explain to you in a plain, simple and rational way, what the Quran teaches: "… that which is easy to understand…" HQ 54:17.

HQ 7:3 "Follow O men the revelation given unto you from your Lord, and follow not as friends or protectors other than Him. Little it is that ye remember of admonition." And God by His Words doth prove and establishes His Truth, however much the sinners may hate it.

Dear reader, then which of the gifts of thy Lord will you dispute? This is a warning as given earlier to mankind by all righteous prophets and men. The Judgement Day that has to come draws nigh. Do you find this book strange? Will you laugh and not weep, wasting your time in vanities? Now you are invited to prostrate yourself and adore Him, by your reason.

Don't you think that this is the true end of Revelation and the true attitude when we understand the world, nature, history and the working of God's Plan?

HQ 39:18 "Those who listen to the Word and follow the best (meaning) in it; those are the ones whom God has guided, and those are the ones endowed with understanding."

It is expected that those who are spiritually dead will, by some chance, hear the Call and Message of God. May God bless you.

Once again a repeat of our prophet's prayer:

May Allah (God) make

Wisdom your Capital

Reason the force of your Religion

Love your Foundation

Longing your Vehicle

Remembrance of Allah your constant Pleasure

Trust your Treasure

Mourning your Companion

Knowledge your Arm

Patience your Robe

Conviction your Strength

Poverty your Pride

Contentment your Booty

Asceticism your Profession
Holy war your Ethics
Truthfulness your Intercessor
Obedience your Argument
And Prayers your supreme Pleasure. Amen

You lack knowledge if you do not make use of your intellect. Do not be swayed by your passions. You lack guidance if you are impatient for control of the fruits of revelation, and spiritual insight will not reach you, if you reject Faith and Revelation. Do realise that in the spiritual world as in the physical world, there is constant progress for the live ones; they are spiritually dead who are content to stagnate with habitual ways, many of them evil and leading to perdition.

If we believe in a soul at all—the very foundation of religion—we must believe in a future after death without which the soul has no meaning. Do not be a coward and use your intelligence and reasoning power to reap the spiritual good which your knowledge, instruction, and experience entitle you to attain. But even then God's Mercy comes to the cowards as long as the door of repentance remains open. It is now your duty to teach, instruct, preach to others what you believe in.

A reminder: The logical conclusion to the evolution of religious history is a non-sectarian, non-racial, non-doctrinal, universal religion, which Islam claims to be. For Islam is, simply, submission to the will of God. This implies:

1. Faith
2. Doing right, being an example to others to do right, and having the power to see that the right prevails.
3. Eschewing wrong, being an example to others to eschew wrong and having the power to see that wrong and injustice are defeated. Islam therefore lives not for itself,

but for mankind. The People of the Book (Christians and Jews), if only they had faith, would be Muslims, for they have been prepared for Islam; so also all other faiths as preached by their prophets.

The original and true words of their preaching have been lost, misquoted, and maligned for worldly gain. Unfortunately, there is no faith, but it can never harm those who carry the burner of Faith and Right, which has been, must be, and will always be victorious.

"Nay, here are signs self-evident in the hearts of those endowed with knowledge[8]: And none but the unjust reject Our Signs" HQ 29:49.

To men so endowed with God's revelations and Signs this is self-evident. They commend themselves to their hearts, minds and understanding. Fear God, O ye men of understanding, who have believed! For God hath indeed sent down to you a Message.

There is no excuse for us to go astray, seeing that God in His Infinite Mercy has explained to us His Message by His many Signs in nature around us and clearly by means of the human teachers/apostles whom He has sent for our instruction. One God, the one Teacher and one class—the earth, nay, the whole universe. Therefore, the lesson has to be the same by all teachers to all mankind. One should not feel shy or be too proud to accept the One Truth in order to comprehend, the knowledge of religion.

HQ 21:107. "We sent thee (Prophet Muhammad) as a Mercy for all creation." There is no question now of race or nation, of a 'chosen people', or the 'seed of Abraham' or the 'seed of David'; or a Hindu Arya-varta; of Jew or

---

[8] Knowledge here means both power and judgement in discerning the value of truth, and acquaintance with previous revelations. It implies both literal and spiritual insight.

Gentile, Arab or Ajam (Persian), Turk or Tajik, European or Asiatic, white or brown; Aryan, Semitic, Mongolian, or African; or American, Australian, or Polynesian. To all men and creatures (other than men who have any spiritual responsibility), the principles apply universally.

The culmination of God's Revelation is in the Quran, which confirms previous scriptures, corrects the errors which men introduced into them, and explains many points in detail for all who seek the right way to worship and serve God—whether they inherit the previous Books or not. The Message is universal.

Preserve the dignity of man, with soul erect; the Universal Plan will all protect. The test is of man's acknowledgement of the greatness of God on every occasion, whether he pays attention to the voice of his conscience or ignores it. When he is confronted with logical argument, does he surrender to the Truth or go against it? When there is a choice between ego and Truth, does he accept the Truth or become an egotist? Reason it out for yourself.

Islam is itself a precious privilege. By accepting it we confer no favour on its preacher or any community. If the acceptance is from the heart, it is a great favour done to those who accept that the Light of God has entered their hearts and they have received guidance.

HQ 49:17says: "…Count not our Islam as a favour upon me (Prophet Muhammad). Nay God has conferred a favour upon you that He has guided you to the Faith, if ye be true and sincere."

Things of the highest moment have been explained in the Quran from various points of view by means of parables and similitudes drawn from nature and from our ordinary daily lives. But whatever the explanation, however convincing it may be to men who earnestly seek after Truth, those who deliberately turn their backs to Truth can find nothing convincing. In their eyes the explanations are merely vain talk or false arguments. The only people who will gain from spiritual teaching are those who bring their minds to it, who believe and submit their wills to the Will of God.

This is the central doctrine of Islam.

What could it be but our rank ingratitude and failure to use the understanding and reasoning which God has given us?

The mission of Islam:

1. The God about whom it preaches is not an exclusive God. He is the Lord of the worlds: To any person, of whatever faith, He is your God, as well as mine.
2. Our Faith is not a question of words; it is deeds which decide. Each one of us has personal responsibility for our own conduct.
3. There is no reason for contention whatsoever, when we preach Unity, Truth, and the Hereafter.
4. If you have doubts, the final arbiter is God, and His Throne is the goal of Islam.

God makes the soul and gives it order, proportion, and relative perfection, in order to adopt it for the particular circumstances in which it has to live its life. He breathes into the soul an understanding of what sin, impiety and wrongdoing are, and including in the particular circumstances in which man may be placed. This is the most precious gift of all to man—the faculty to distinguish right and wrong.

After one sees the evidence of God in the Heavens and on Earth this internal evidence of God's Goodness is regarded as the greatest of all. By these various tokens, as seen and understood, man should learn that his success, his prosperity and his salvation depend upon himself, on his keeping his soul pure as God made it; and his failure, his decline, his perdition is the result of his soiling his soul by choosing evil.

This poor surmise of the Holy Quran addressed to the whole world and in particular to Christians/Nicea Councilists/Trinitarians, is an argument of the most searching nature. Examine your own souls; see if you do not really find something unusual in all of God's True Revelations! If you do and yet you reject it, what a terrible responsibility fastens itself on you. Could anything be more foolish or more misguided than to reject a Revelation which is transforming the whole world?

Do not think that you are doing me a favour by accepting Islam, or that I am taking credit for it. If your acceptance is from the heart, then it is a great favour from God that you have received guidance.

HQ 2:269. "…But none will grasp the Message but men of understanding."

Of no profit will this counsel be to you unless you use your God-given reason and decide for yourself that God, the One and Only, is our Lord and to Him will all humankind return.

Man's insolence leads to two results:

1. Self-destruction through self-misleading.
2. A false example or false guidance to others. The righteous man must therefore test human example by the question:

a) Is God's guidance behind it?

b) Does it lead to righteousness?

Flouting of God and His Truth answers the first question in the negative, and conduct which turns back from the eternal principle of Right answers the second.

God's highest gift to man is that He has furnished a clear distinction between right and wrong in His revelations, which teaches us the true significance of our eternal Future. Those who do not use this distinction will be full of woe when the judgement comes, for God gives full warning at all times to all people.

(Refer HQ25:63-74).

The righteous are known in the environment of this world by the following 12 deeds:

1. Walking on earth in humility.
2. Addressing the ignorant with peace.
3. Spending the night in adoration of their Lord.
4. Those who say "Our Lord, avert from us the wrath of Hell."
5. Those who, when they spend, are not extravagant nor niggardly.
6. Those who invoke not with God any other god.
7. Those who slay not such life as God has made sacred except for just cause.
8. Those who commit not fornication.
9. Those who do not bear witness to falsehood.
10. Those who avoid futility honourably.
11. Those who pay attention when they are admonished with the signs of their Lord.
12. Those who pray "Our Lord! Grant unto us wives and offspring who will be the comfort of our eyes." Let us recapitulate the virtues of the true servants of God:

1. They are humble and forbearing to those below them in spiritual worth.
2. They are constantly, by adoration, in touch with God.
3. They always remember the Judgement in the Hereafter.
4. They are moderate in all things.

5. They avoid treason to God, to their fellow creatures, and to themselves.
6. They give a wide berth not only to falsehood, but also to futility.
7. They pay attention both in mind and manner, to the signs of their Lord.
8. Their ambition is to bring up their families in righteousness and to lead in all good.

A fine code of individual and social ethics, a ladder of spiritual development, open to all.

ON THE TAURAT (JEWISH LAW)

The Taurat is frequently referred to in the Quran. It is well to have clear ideas as to what it actually means. Vaguely we may say it was the Jewish Scripture. It is mentioned with honour as having been, in its purity, a true revelation from God.

To translate it by the words "The Old Testament" is obviously wrong. The "Old Testament" is a Christian term, applied to a body of Jewish records. The Protestants and the Roman Catholics are not agreed precisely as to the number of records to be included in the canon of the "Old Testament". They use the term in contradistinction to the "New Testament", whose composition we shall discuss in Appendix II.

Nor is it correct to translate the Taurat as "Pentateuch", a Greek term meaning the "Five Books". These are the first five books of the "Old Testament", known as Genesis, Exodus, Leviticus, Numbers and Deuteronomy. They contain a semi-historical and legendary history of the world from the Creation to the time of the arrival of the Jews in the Promised Land. There are in them some beautiful idylls but there are also stories of incest, fraud, cruelty, and treachery, not always disapproved. A great part of the Mosaic Law is embodied in this narrative. The books are traditionally ascribed to Moses, but it is certain that they were not written by Moses or in an age either contemporary with Moses or within an appreciable distance of time from Moses. They were in their present form probably compiled some time after the return of the Jews from the Babylonian Captivity. The decree of Cyrus permitting such return was in 536 B.C. Some books now included in the Old Testament, such as Haggai, Zecharaiah and Malachi were admittedly written after the return from the captivity, Malachi being as late as 420 – 397 B.C. The compilers of the Pentateuch of course used some ancient material: some of that material is actually named. Egyptian and Chaldaean terms are relics of local colour and contemporary documents.

But there are some ludicrous slips, which show that the compilers did not always understand their material. Modern criticism distinguishes two distinct sources among the documents of different dates used by the editors. For the sake of brevity and convenience they may be called a) Jehovistic and

b) Elohistic. Then there are later miscellaneous interpolations. They sometimes overlap and sometimes contradict each other. Logically speaking, the Book of Joshua, which describes the entry into the Promised Land, should be bracketed with the Pentateuch, and many writers speak of the six books together as the Hexateuch (Greek term for Six Books).

The Apocrypha contain certain Books which are not admitted as Canonical in the English Bible. But the early Christians received them as part of the Jewish Scriptures, and the Council of Trent (A.D. 1545-1563) seems to have recognized the greater part of them as Canonical. The statement in 2 Esdras (about the first century A.D.) that the law was burnt and Ezra (say about 458-457 B.C.) was inspired to rewrite it, is probably true as to the historical fact that the law was lost, and that what we have now is no earlier than the time of Ezra, and some of it a good deal later.

So far we have spoken of the Christian view of the Old Testament. What is the Jewish view? The Jews divide their Scripture into three parts. (1) the Law (Torah), (2) the Prophets (Nebiim), and (3) the Writings (Rethubim). The corresponding Arabic words would be: (1) Taurat (2) Nabiyin, and (3) Rutub. This division was probably current in the time of Jesus. In Luke xxiv. 44 Jesus refers to the Law and the Prophets as summing up the whole scripture. In the Old Testament Book, II. Chronicles xxxiv. 30, the reference to the Book of the Covenant must be to the Torah or the original law. This is interesting, as the Quran terms "Old Testament" and "New Testament" are substitutes for the older terms "Old Covenant" and "New Covenant." The Samaritans, who claim to be the real Children of Israel and disavow the Jews as schismatics from their Law of Moses, only recognize the Pentateuch, of which they have their own version slightly different from that in the Old Testament.

The view of the school of Higher Criticism is radically destructive. According to Renan it is doubtful whether Moses was not a myth. Two versions of Sacred History existed, different in language, style and spirit, and they were combined together in the reign of Hezekiah (B.C. 727-697). This forms the greater part of the Pentateuch as it exists today, excluding the greater part of Deuteronomy and Leviticus. In the reign of Josaiah about 622 B.C., certain priests and scribes (with Jeremiah the prophet) promulgated a new code, pretending they had found it in the Temple. (II. Kings xxii.8) This law (Torah=Taurat) was the basis of Judaism, the new religion then founded in Palestine. This was further completed by the sacerdotal and Levitical Torah, compiled under the inspiration of Ezekiel, say, about 575 B.C., and contained mainly in the Book of Leviticus, with scattered fragments in Exodus, Numbers, and Joshua. We are entitled to accept the general results of a scientific examination of documents, probabilities, and dates, even though we rejects the premise which we believe to be false, viz., that God 1 not send inspired Books through inspired Prophets. We believe that Moses existed; that he was an inspired man of God; that he gave a message which was afterwards distorted or lost; that attempts were made by Israel at various times to reconstruct that message; and that the Taurat as we have it is (in view of the statement in 2 Edras) no earlier than the middle of the fifth century B.C.

The primitive Torah must have been in Hebrew, but there is no Hebrew manuscript of the Old Testament which can be dated with certainty earlier than 916 A.D. Hebrew ceased to be a spoken language with the Jews during or after the Captivity, and by the time we come to the period of Jesus, most cultivated Hebrews used the Greek language, and others used Aramaic (including Syriac and Chaldee), Latin, or local dialects. There were also Arabic versions. For historical purposes the most important versions were the Greek version, known as the Septuagint, and the Latin version, known as the Vulgate. The Septuagint was supposed to have been prepared by 70 or 72 Jews (Latin, septuaginta = seventy) working independently and at different times, the earliest portion dating from about 284 B.C. This version was used by Jews of Alexandria and the Hellenized Jews who were spread over all parts of the Roman Empire. The Vulgate was a Latin translation made by the celebrated Father of the Christian Church, St. Jerome, from Hebrew, early in the fifth century A.D., superseding the older Latin versions. Neither the Septuagint nor the Vulgate have an absolutely fixed or certain text. The present standard text of the Vulgate as accepted by the Roman Catholic Church was issued by Pope Clement VIII (A.D. 1592–1605).

It will be seen therefore that there is no standard text of the Old Testament in its Hebrew form. The versions differ from each other frequently in minor particulars and sometimes in important particulars. The Pentateuch itself is only a small portion of the Old Testament. It is in narrative form, and includes the laws and regulations associated with the name of Moses, but probably compiled and edited from older sources by Exra (or Esdras Arabic, 'Uzair) in the 5th century B.C. As Renan remarks in the preface to his History of the People of Isreal, the "definite constitution of Judaism" may be dated only from the time of Ezra. The very early Christians were divided into two parties. One was a Judaizing party, which wished to remain in adherence to the Jewish laws and customs while recognizing the mission of Jesus. The other, led by Paul, broke away from Jewish customs and traditions. Ultimately Pauline Christianity won. But both parties recognised the Old Testament in its present form (in one or another of its varying versions) as Scripture. It was the merit of Islam that it pointed out that as scripture it was of no value, although it recognised Moses as an inspired apostle and his original Law as having validity in his period until it was superseded. In its criticism of the Jewish position it said in effect: "You have lost your original Law; even what you have now as its substitute, you do not honestly follow; is it not better, now that an inspired Teacher is living among you, that you should follow him rather than quibble over uncertain texts?"

But the Jews in the Apostle's time (and since) went a great deal by the Talmud, or a body of oral exposition, reduced to writing in different Schools of in Talmiz, "disciple" or "student." The Talmudists took the divergent texts of the Old Testament and in interpreting them by a mass of traditional commentary and legendary lore, evolved a standard body of teaching. The Talmudists are of special interest to us, as, in the sixth century A.D., just before the preaching of Islam, they evolved the Massorah, which may be regarded as the body of authoritative Jewish Hadith, to which references are to be found in passages addressed to the Jews in the Quran.

The first part of the Talmud is called the Mishna—a collection of traditions and decisions prepared by the Rabbi Judah about 150 A.D. He summed up the results of a great mass of previous rabbinical writings. The Mishna is the "Second Law" : Compare the Arabic Than-in=second. "It bound heavy burdens, grievous to be borne, and laid them on men's shoulders": Matt xxiii. 4,

There were also many Targums or paraphrases of the Law among the Jews. "Targum" is connected in root with the Arabic word Tarjama, "he translated." There were many Targums, mostly in Aramaic, and they constituted the teaching of the Law to the masses of the Jewish people.

The correct translation of the Taurat is therefore "The Law." In its original form it was promulgated by Moses, and is recognised in Islam as having been an inspired Book. But it was lost before Islam was preached. But what passed as "The Law" with the Jews in the Apostle's time was the mass of traditional writing which I have tried to review in this Appendix.

Authorities: Encyclopaedia Britannica, "Bible": Helps to the Study of the Bible, Oxford University Press: A.F. Kirkpatrick, Divine Library of the Old Testament, C. E. Hammond, Outlines of Textual Criticism, E. Renan, History of Israel, G. I. Moore, Literature of the Old Testament, and the bibliography therein (Home University Library), Sir Fredric Kenyon, The Story of the Bible, 1936.

ON THE INJIL (GOSPEL)

Just as the Taurat is not the Old Testament, or the Pentateuch, as now received by the Jews and Christians, so the Injil mentioned in the Quran is certainly not the New Testament, and it is not the four Gospels as now received by the Christian Church, but an original Gospel which was promulgated by Jesus, as the Taurat was promulgated by Moses and the Quran by Muhammad Mustafa.

The New Testament as now received consists of a) four Gospels with varying contents (Matthew, Mark, Luke, and John); and other miscellaneous matters viz., (b) the Acts of the Apostles (probably written by Luke and purporting to describe the progress of the Christian Church under St. Peter and St. Paul from the supposed Crucifixion of Jesus to about 61 A.D.); (c) twenty-one Letters or Epistles (the majority written by St. Paul to various churches or individuals, but a few written by other Disciples, and of a general nature) ; and (d) the Book of Revelation or Apocalypse (ascribed to St. John, and containing mystic visions and prophecies, of which it is difficult to understand the meaning).

As Prof. F. C. Burkitt remarks (Canon of the New Testament), it is an odd miscellany. "The four biographies of Jesus Christ…are not all independent of each other, and neither of them was intended by its writer to form one of a quartet. But they are all put side by side, unharmonised, one of them being actually imperfect at the end, and one being only the first volume of a larger work." All this body of unmethodical literature was casual in its nature. No wonder, because the early Christians expected the end of the world very soon. The four canonical Gospels were only four out of many, and some others besides the four have survived. Each writer just wrote down some odd sayings of the Master that he recollected. Among the miracles described there is only one which is described in all the four Gospels, and others were described and believed in other Gospels, which are not mentioned in any of the four canonical Gospels. Some of the Epistles contain expositions of doctrine, but this has been interpreted differently by different Churches. There must have been hundreds of such Epistles, and not all the Epistles now received as canonical were always so received or intended to be so received. The Apocalypse also was not the only one in the field. There were others. They were prophecies of "things which must shortly come to pass" ; they could not have been meant for long preservation, " for the time is at hand."

When were these four Gospels written ? By the end of the second century A.D. they were in existence, but it does not follow that they had been selected by that date to form a canon. They were merely pious productions comparable to Dean Farrar's Life of Christ. There were other Gospels besides. And further, the writers of two of them, Mark and Luke, were not among the Twelve Disciples "called" by Jesus. About the Gospel of St. John there is much controversy as to authorship, date, and even as to whether it was all written by one person. Clement of Rome (about 97 A.D.) and Polycarp (about 112 A.D.) quote sayings of Jesus in a form different from those found in the present canonical Gospels. Polycarp (Epistle, vii) inveighs much against men "who pervert the sayings of the Lord to their own lusts," and he wants to turn "to the Word handed down to us from the beginning."

Thus referring to a Book (or a Tradition) much earlier than the four orthodox Gospels. An Epistle of St. Barnabas and an Apocalypse of St. Peter were recognised by Presbyter Clement of Alexandria (flourished about 180 A.D.). The Apocalypse of St. John, which is a part of the present Canon in the West, forms no part of the Peshitta (Syriac) versions of the Eastern Christians, which was produced about 411- 433 A.D. and which was used by the Nestorian Christians. It is probable that the Peshitta was the version (or an Arabic form of it) used by the Christians in Arabia in the time of the Apostle. The final form of the New Testament canon for the West was fixed in the fourth century A.D. (say, about 367 A.D.) by the Athanasius and the Nicene creed. The beautiful Codex Sinaiticus which was acquired for the British Museum in 1934, and is one of the earliest complete manuscripts of the Bible, may be dated about the fourth century. It is written in the Greek language. Fragments of unknown Gospels have also been discovered, which do not agree with the received canonical Gospels.

The Injil (Greek, Evangel=Gospel) spoken of by the Quran is not the New Testament. It is not the four Gospels now received as canonical. It is the single Gospel which, Islam teaches, was revealed to Jesus, and which he taught. Fragments of it survive in the received canonical Gospels and in some others, of which traces survive (e.g., the Gospel of Childhood or the Nativity, the Gospel of St. Barnabas, etc.). Muslims are therefore right in respecting the present Bible (New Testament and Old Testament), though they reject the peculiar doctrines taught by orthodox Christianity or Judaism. They claim to be in the true tradition of Abraham, and therefore all that is of value in the older revelations, it is claimed, is incorporated in the teaching of the Last of the Prophets.

In V.85 we are told that nearest in love to the Believers among the People of the Book are the Christians. I do not agree that this does not apply to modern Christians "because they are practically atheists or freethinkers." I think that Christian thought like the world's thought) has learnt a great deal from the protest of Islam against priest domination, class domination, and sectarianism, and its insistence on making this life pure and beautiful while we are in it. We must stretch a friendly hand to all who are sincere and in sympathy with our ideals.

Authorities: The first two mentioned for Appendix I, and in addition: Prof. F. C. Burkitt. On the Cannon of the New Testament, in Religion, June 1934, the Journal of Transactions of the Society for promoting the Study of Religions; R. W. Mackay, Rise and Progress of Christianity; G. R. S. Mead, The Gospel and the Gospels; B. W. Bacon, Making of the New Testament, with its Bibliography; Sir Frederic Kenyon, The Story of the Bible; R. Hone, The Apocryphal New Testament, London 1820: H. I Bell and T. C. Skeat, Fragments of an Unknown Gospel and other Christian Papyri, published by the British Museum, 1935. See also chapter 15 of Gibbon's Decline and Fall of the Roman Empire, where the genesis of the early churches and sects in the Roman Empire is briefly reviewed.

9 798889 322996 7